INSHALLAH UNITED

INSHALLAH UNITED

A STORY OF FAITH & FOOTBALL

NOORUDDEAN CHOUDRY

Harper
North

HarperNorth
Windmill Green
24 Mount Street
Manchester M2 3NX

A division of
HarperCollins*Publishers*
1 London Bridge Street
London SE1 9GF

www.harpercollins.co.uk

HarperCollins*Publishers*
Macken House, 39/40 Mayor Street Upper
Dublin 1, D01 C9W8, Ireland

First published by HarperNorth in 2023
This edition published by HarperNorth in 2024

1 3 5 7 9 10 8 6 4 2

A catalogue record for this book
is available from the British Library

HB ISBN: 978-0-00-852223-0
PB ISBN: 978-0-00-852226-1

Printed and bound in the UK using 100%
renewable electricity at CPI Group (UK) Ltd

This book contains FSC™ certified paper and other controlled
sources to ensure responsible forest management.

For more information visit: www.harpercollins.co.uk/green

To my mum, Tahira. Thank you for every single sacrifice you made for us and all the love and strength you provide. You're the root and we're the branches. We can never repay you, but I hope we make you proud.

'I feel close to the rebelliousness of the youth here. Perhaps time will separate us, but nobody can deny that here, behind the windows of Manchester, there is an insane love of football, of celebration and of music.'

'It is important not to say that a Muslim is "moderate". What does "moderate" mean anyway? Does it mean that Islam is an extreme religion? This is latent provocation. We do not have to paint everybody with the same brush. That is the danger I think.'

Eric Cantona

CONTENTS

PROLOGUE

Bismillah

I don't understand football fans who arrive at a game at the latest possible moment. Like, if you gave them a magic switch that instantly transported them from their sofa to their seat just before kickoff, they would snap your hand off quicker than you could say 'hot Bovril'. It makes zero sense to me. It's like wanting to immediately skip to Christmas Day with your choc-laden advent calendar unopened or celebrating Eid al-Fitr without a single day of Ramadan. What is the joy in anything without the anticipation? So much of life is ultimately an anti-climax, so why not relish the great wind of excitement that carries you there?

I love everything about matchday – even the bits I don't. Maybe it's because I missed out on the formative dad/lad experience of going to the game with my old man, but I'm never giddier than when I'm making my way to Old Trafford. Especially if it's a night game, and especially if it's so cold that you're breathing out pretend cigarette smoke. Those are my favourite nights. I don't even care if it's raining; in fact, I think I prefer a mild drizzle. The dazzling red and white lights spill all over the floor and make it feel even more special. Forget Blackpool illuminations, give me Old Trafford when it's pissing it down and the end of your nose is dripping like a leaky tap. Only Wilmslow Road's Curry Mile, with its assault of colourful neon, looks better on a wet night.

Whenever an international Red asks me for any tips about visiting Old Trafford, I always offer them two pieces of advice. Firstly, take out your AirPods – this is a journey you may well experience a number of times if you're lucky, but never again for the first time, so leave all your senses fully open to savouring it properly. Secondly, get off the tram or bus far earlier than the closest stop. Make your walk to the ground as long as your age and abilities allow. Because that's when you experience the true sense of pilgrimage. The slow build-up of smells and sounds and human traffic that culminate outside the stadium. Whether it's the sizzle and unmistakable whiff of frying onions, or the manic street preachings of Red News and United We Stand fanzine sellers, it's the matchday ritual that's the thing, not the actual game.

Now, I won't say going to a United game is exactly a divine experience – so as to neatly tie together the two themes of this book – that would be hack and fundamentally untrue. I don't walk to the mosque in fervent anticipation of the Imam producing a world-class performance that we'll all rave about afterwards. I don't look forward to catching up with the other prayers later on Mufti of the Day presented by Sheikh Ghari Al-Lineker. And we don't all join in with the Muezzin when he recites the Call to Prayer, holding our keffiyehs aloft, and giving out a big cheer when he's done. That said, there are at least some similarities, and they have far more to do with the journey than the destination. It's the genuine sense of brother and sisterhood that comes from experiencing a collective focus and belief. Faith is a personal condition; religion is a communal act.

I like walking to Friday prayers for the same reason I like walking to the game: it gives me an overwhelming sense of belonging. People of all backgrounds and races and nationalities and cultures are all joined together by at least one singular identity that unites them all. We're not all the same and there's a heart-swelling beauty in that. Whether it's mosque or match, I love the way the congregation starts to funnel into a bigger and bigger mass as you meander along the streets and walkways. More and more people join your parade, all different but all the same, until you reach your full number – to watch Bruno Fernandes shank an overhit pass out of play, or a Muslim elder pull a frown when he hears change dropping into the collection box instead of something that folds.

I hate it when I arrive late at Old Trafford, or halfway through the sermon at mosque. I'm flustered. My head and my heart are not where they need to be. And I feel like I've missed out on the most important bit – doing it together. Walking together, arriving together, *believing* together. Fundamentally, I think we all want to belong to something bigger than ourselves. To have an identity that resonates with others and makes us whole. Thank Allah, I do.

1.

ALWAYS A RED, NEARLY A BLUE

It's still there, the Egerton Inn. A traditional-looking watering hole tucked away in a quiet corner of Cheetham Hill, right next to the local primary school. It's literally a feeble child's crayon throw away: cask and climbing frame side-by-side in the worst piece of urban planning this side of Strangeways. I'm not sure what came first, chicken and egg I suppose, but it was (and still is) a weirdly inappropriate juxtaposition. You've got little kids running about in the playground just yards away from seasoned imbibers in the beer garden. And I'm casting no aspersions on any Egerton regulars past or present, but anyone sat outside on one of the wooden benches basically had an unobstructed front-row view of a mass of oblivious kids. Thankfully, the space between pint and play area is safely boarded up these days so it's less nonce-friendly, but back when I attended Cravenwood County Primary (now an 'academy', whatever that means) in the 1980s, there was but a flimsy wire fence between pisshead and child.

Not long before, I joined my two sisters at Cravenwood in the 1984 nursery intake. Cravenwood's grand old red-brick building was demolished and replaced with a 'modern' build: boxy, soulless and bland. Imagine replacing Hogwarts with Wernham Hogg (you know, out of The Office) and you get the picture. I only knew of the previous building from my sisters' old class photographs and some remaining remnants on the perimeter of the new school, slowly eroding half-walls they just forgot to demolish. I was fascinated by those red-brick piles as a kid, especially as there was a rumour going around that one of the walls had fallen on and killed an ex-pupil and her ghost still roamed the school corridors.

It's bizarre how memories work. If only they were like *Match of the Day*, condensing all of the important bits into a highlights package and discarding all the throw-ins and other pointless guff. But it's not like that at all – for me at least – which is a pity. For instance, I couldn't tell you the first time I went to a music gig or who was playing. Or the first time I visited London and why. Or the first time I did a successful Walk the Dog with my gold Coca-Cola yoyo (but it *was* a gold Coca-Cola yoyo). I can't even say for sure what my first game at Old Trafford was, although I'm pretty certain we were playing Villa and the ground was more impressive than the game. What I am almost certain that I recall – and it would be contested by my mum and most scientific journals – is my own circumcision as a wee baby. (There's a small chance it was actually my younger brother's snip and I was so traumatised by it that I've remembered it as my own, but I doubt it.) It's strange what stays with you and how it morphs into something else in your head. Like, I have fond and distinct memories of how I developed a weird little friendship of sorts with a scruffy-looking old timer at the Egerton. Through the fence of the playground, I'd see him sitting outside the pub making funny faces at me, gesticulating wildly and then laughing his head off as I mimicked him. I know it's bad now, but at the time he was like a peculiarity: an adult who was drunk but it was okay and safe because he was behind a fence. It almost felt like looking through an enclosure at Chester Zoo.

That was the playground where I first got madly into football. As in playing. It's funny how you start kicking a ball for the first time and soon every other playground pursuit melts away into irrelevance. Tag no longer cuts it – especially when certain individuals (naming no names, Amanda) just hog the den so they can't be 'it'. You tire of the one-trick wonder of swings and seesaws, and even running around wearing just the hood of your duffle coat like you're Superman eventually loses its charm. Because now, and forevermore, there is football. Chaotic, crowded, everyone-chase-the-ball-in-unison, football. Limitless hordes of us playing with no pitch markings, no formations, no rules (apart from hand ball) and definitely no one arsed with keeping score. At that age, you've got boundless energy and an innate desire to possess whatever everyone else wants, so a flyaway ball with a spasmodic relationship with the laws of physics is ideal.

We used to play on 'bottom pitch' – the general use concrete playground outside the school building – because 'top pitch' was for *proper* matches. So our games of football, such as they were, would be constantly interrupted by skipping ropes, hula hoops, hopscotch and Simon Says. It would be great if Simon could have said 'get out of the way, we're trying to play football'. The promised land of top pitch was adjacent to bottom pitch but on a higher level – up the stairs on one side and up the slope on the other. Unlike bottom pitch, top pitch was an actual football pitch. There were no clear markings as such, but the sandy gravel surface was at least the shape of a football pitch and most importantly had proper goals – posts, crossbars, the lot. They even went clang if you hit them. It was basically our Wembley: the hallowed turf (yellowy dust) compared to our overcrowded, stony scrap heap with literal jumpers for goalposts.

I don't know why top pitch was saved for 'special'. Special never came and therefore it was hardly ever used. And what were they worried about anyway? It wasn't grass that would get muddied and ruined by a hoard of size-12 velcro trainers. The only damage we'd cause would be to our own knees if we fell over, and that happened enough on the concrete. Top pitch being out of bounds was a sham if you ask me – just rules for rules' sake. In fairness, I should have really taken it up with the authorities (teachers and dinner ladies) back then instead of moaning about it here. But let me just say, if you're a teacher (or dinner lady) reading this, and you have the authority on playground duty to allow kids to access *your* equivalent of top pitch, don't be such a jobsworth and bloody let them. Let those kids roam free. Anyway, I digress. As most of us only lived around the corner from the school, we'd end up climbing over the locked gates and playing on top pitch on weekends anyway. So in that sense at least, fuck the police. Or more like 'So there, miss,' as it was Cravenwood not Compton.

I wasn't trying to be anyone when I first started playing football at school. It's not like I was weaving past other kids imagining I was Gordon Strachan, or going into crunching tackles like the second coming of Remi Moses. That all came later. The only obsession I had with football up until around eight or nine years old was playing it. I didn't pay that much attention to games on telly and unlike most footie-mad kids my age, I had no allegiance to a particular club passed down through generations. Both my parents were born and brought up in Pakistan – Dad in Sahiwal and Mum in nearby Arifwala – and they had neither the time nor inclination to take up a new interest, adding Bryan Robson's injury record to their numerous concerns. They were a little bit more preoccupied with assimilating to a new country and bringing up three and then four and then five kids in difficult conditions. My dad had just enough passable knowledge about football to hold down a conversation with a customer in his shop about the game last night, without knowing who was playing, what the score was, or whether there was actually a game last night.

As José Mourinho might have put it, I had no 'football heritage' to speak of. No one to take me to my first game or regale me with tales of seeing Law, Best and Charlton or to pass down old matchday programmes and badges. We didn't even have neighbours who were into football – or neighbours at all for that matter. I lived the entire duration of my formative years in an isolated flat above a shopping precinct. I'm not sure it was really meant to be a flat where people lived, more a space for commercial use. Next door was a dental surgery with the exact same layout as us; the equivalent of the small bedroom I shared with my brother was the dentist's back office. In fact, our only real neighbours were occasional goths, bored arsonists and dead people in the graveyard opposite us, behind Woolworths. I didn't even have any uncles or aunties or older cousins who could ease me into supporting United, City or whoever, on account of them living 4,000 miles away in Pakistan.

But this was Manchester, and that meant football would come to me.

I often wonder what would have transpired had my dad settled in a different part of the country, before my mum joined him over here and they started a family together. There are so many aspects of my personality and whole identity that are intrinsically linked to that quirk of circumstance. It's fundamental to everything about me: being northern, working-class, a Manc, a United fan. Everything I am, barring my race and religion, could have been hugely different had my dad started his new life in Bradford or Leicester or Glasgow or Tower Hamlets. I don't know if I'd be into the same music or fashion or even have the same politics. I appreciate the same could be said of anyone, but for immigrants to a new country there is a massive element of starting again. You don't lose your culture or familial roots, but you *do* gain a whole new set of identifiers and influences. For instance, your family could be seen as pretty well-to-do and upwardly mobile 'back home', but in a new country you're back on that bottom rung. You can have middle-class pretensions, but your kids are still growing up financially, socially and environmentally working class. I'm just relieved I grew up Manc and not somewhere they loved rugby.

To think I could have been writing this wearing red trousers and a gilet, but I didn't grow up a rugby fan and this book isn't called *Harlequins Inshallah*. I'm a football-mad Manc and it was written in the stars. But kismet aside, the lack of inherited allegiance made me a blank canvas. I couldn't be one of those saddo neutrals who just want 'football to be the real winner'. This was towards the late 1980s and neither Manchester club was pulling up any trees. City were bad – flitting between the bottom half of the table and the old Second Division – but United weren't much better. A lot of fans were starting to lose patience with the manager at the time, an authoritarian Scot by the name of Alex Ferguson. The point is there was no obvious and convenient bandwagon to jump on if you had an 061 number. Indeed, the only clear choice for glory supporting in the *Now That's What I Call Music 11* era involved taking Joe Le Taxi across the East Lancs Road to Merseyside.

Liverpool had been the dominant force in English football for ages and certainly all of my short life. They were relentless. So established and transcendental was their success that even my dad knew to moan about them winning again while counting out change. He was unlikely to be wrong. And don't assume that just because I was on the wrong side of the civic divide that supporting Liverpool wasn't a possibility. There are many stereotypes about Asians in this country that are lazy, offensive, bigoted and plainly untrue, but one that's not spoken about enough is glory-supporting. Every loyal and committed Asian fan knows at least three that are as fair weather as they come. Perhaps it is born of the diaspora's instinct to fit in, or maybe it's because we have enough natural melanin to withstand all that reflected glory. Either way, it's a thing. I know many Liverpool-supporting Asians with a Manc twang from that era. Taxi drivers are the worst. There is no truer bellwether for which way the football winds are blowing than the club a taxi driver claims to support at any given time. They were all Red and now they're all Blue. Utterly shameless and no stars from me.

Although nearly all the boys and a few of the girls played football at our school, we only had a handful of actual proper football fans in our class who supported a particular club. Cravenwood didn't have a school uniform back then and so we could wear pretty much whatever we pleased – apart from football colours. That's right, we were treated like boozed-up aggro-hunting cokeheads trying to get into Tiger Tiger just for wearing football tops. Despite the bouncers/teachers and their strict anti-hooligan policy, two bona fide football fans sat at my very table. They were Terence Johnson and Thomas Wright – one Red, one Blue. Little did either of them know that they held my football fate and future happiness in their grubby PVA glue-covered hands.

Terence sat next to me and we were really good mates. He was impressed with me being such a good drawer (I could do shading, which was like witchcraft at that age), and for my part I liked the fact that a) he was arguably the cock of the class, although Brendan Vinter was also a strong contender, and b) he had really cool hair. It was the severest of pudding-bowl haircuts, shaved to zero under a perfectly straight 'step'. You see why I was so impressed. He was also especially good at football, which was clearly a big factor in social standing. Thomas was a mate too, but sitting at the opposite end of the table there was a metaphorical and physical chasm between us. Sure we'd happily play with each other if we were in the same group, and I had no problem holding his hand on school trips if partnered together, but it's not like we were sitting-next-to-each-other-in-the-quiet-corner pals or on 'you're really good at shading' terms. He was more a casual acquaintance than a best friend. On the hair front, his was ginger and wiry but that wasn't an issue for me – I didn't see colour.

As for their respective teams, Terence was a City fan while Thomas's allegiance was as red as his hair. And after I casually remarked one day that I didn't have a club of my own, both made it their business to recruit me to their cause. It was like I was a highly sought-after Bosman signing before Bosman was even a thing. There was a tug-of-war to secure my loyalty and of course I was flattered to be linked to such impressive classmates. In fairness, they both made compelling cases. Thomas argued that United were really good and better than City, while Terence countered that City were better than United and really really good. It was certainly a quandary. I think Usman (who sat opposite, next to Dara) might have briefly thrown Liverpool's name into the mix to spice things up further, but it was a tentative approach more than anything and wasn't followed up with a firm offer. It came down to a clear choice – Maine Road or Old Trafford.

Everything else being equal, it should have been City. Terence was a better mate, plus he had Panini spares of the likes of Jason Beckford and Andy Dibble to sweeten the deal. He assured me that they were absolute top-class players and therefore very highly sought after. I can't say I wasn't tempted – they'd go nicely on the front of my drawer next to the Garbage Pail Kids and Knight Rider ones already in situ. And who knows, a nice shiny foil club badge could have pushed me over the edge and have me declare myself a Blue there and then. But for all Terence's perseverance, Thomas was always more persuasive. Not because he was offering me stickers of Jim Leighton or Clayton Blackmore or anything like that. Nor was he making some prophetic case for Fergie eventually turning things around and heralding an unprecedented era of success in the club's storied history. The thing that drew me to Thomas's side was his total and complete obsession for the club he loved.

There's something incredibly appealing about someone with an all-encompassing passion, whether it's football or Dungeons & Dragons or trainspotting or whatever. You might think the object of their affections is pretty lame or trivial, but there is a purity and wholesomeness to their undiluted love that elevates it a little closer to sacred. It suddenly has greater worth. Of course such things can occasionally spill over into weird fanaticism à la Jed Maxwell in *I'm Alan Partridge*, or Royalists who think they can channel Princess Diana and know exactly what she'd think of Meghan Markle. But in general, a nerdy obsession is a beautiful thing. And like most football fans – especially young ones – that's exactly what Thomas had. Ultimately that was the difference. Terence really liked football, but Thomas *loved* it. The way he talked about Manchester United, the way he continually drew their badge over and over again like he was performing a ritual of thanks, the way he surreptitiously wore a Sharp-sponsored top under his jumper – he made being a United fan seem like the most important thing in the world.

Another not insignificant factor that swayed my decision was a poster in the school corridor featuring members of Bobby Robson's England squad – or 'England's No Smoking Team' – imploring us to quit smoking courtesy of the Health Education Council. There was a short summary of each player's career followed by a scary smoking fact like 'You're five times more likely to die from cigarettes than a road accident' (citation needed). Of the 16 or so players telling us that 'pacesetters don't smoke', around three or four of them played for Manchester United, including goalkeeper Gary Bailey and captain Bryan Robson. There were no City players to be seen. That meant either none of the City lot were good enough to play for their country, or worse, they *were* good enough but smoked like chimneys. Either way, it wasn't a good look. It both firmed up my desire to become a Red and helped to put me off cigarettes. Now I know what you may be thinking: why was warning us off smoking such a concern at primary school age? Different times, I suppose. Plus this was Crumpsall in the mid-1980s, it was a bit rough and ready around the edges and we grew up fast. While smoking, apparently.

There was some irony in the fact we were being so strongly urged to stay off nicotine while being hooked onto caffeine at the very same time. It is a memory so absurd that I was initially convinced I'd got it wrong – until corroborated by siblings and friends – but believe it or not, we were served a sweet milky coffee en masse at the end of each and every dinner time. Goodness knows what the thinking was behind this policy to pump us full of Maxwell House but it was gratefully lapped up without question. Maybe we were so malnourished and gaunt-looking that they figured we needed a little boost to make it through the afternoon. Or maybe the teachers fancied a challenge and figured we weren't quite hyper enough without a daily dose of sugar and caffeine. Regardless, I enjoyed that daily lukewarm pick-me-up right through primary school. Maggie Thatcher might have succeeded in snatching our milk, but damn it, she could never take our coffee.

I needed an extra strong cup to steady my nerves the day I told Terence I was rejecting 'Blue Moon' for the 'Manchester United Calypso'. But fair play to him, he was properly sound about it. There was no bitterness and labelling me a good-for-nothing glory hunter. Maybe there was even a part of him that was relieved. I think he quite enjoyed being in the minority supporting City round our way. The 'Manchester is red/Manchester is blue' debate has always been a boring one but it's true that parts of the locality are generally more one than the other. Cheetham Hill, like nearby Salford, is mostly red. Stockport (and surrounding areas) is more blue. Even at that age, there was a sort of inherited cachet that went with going for the less 'fashionable' choice. It was akin to choosing Donatello as your favourite Turtle, or preferring Tygra to Lion-O. I sometimes wonder whether, for all their success in recent years, some of the older City fans miss the days before they were so 'mainstream' and easy to follow. Like there's an inverse credibility to how badly your team does and yet you support them regardless. On second thoughts they probably just enjoy winning stuff and being miles better than us.

Rather than resent my redness, Terence embraced it. He now had two United fans on our table who he could rib and exchange pisstakery with. If anything, he was more vocal and open about being a City fan than before. Like a dormant muscle that needed something to strain against. Or a He-Man that needed a Skeletor. It points to one of the most central and contradictory truisms of football fandom: you want your fiercest rivals to fail, to suffer, to implode before your very eyes and generally be in the mud. But you'd hate for them to not exist, because then a part of you wouldn't exist either. It's the theory of shithouse relativity. Without a team to hate (and by 'hate'

I mean football hate, not real-life hate) any success would just be measured against itself. You'd either win or lose and that'd be that, which would be rubbish. Winning in football is fun, but it only really matters if someone else is mardy about it. Every achievement is relative to someone else's comparative failure. The mad thing is, whoever's momentarily happy or sad in this symbiotic dynamic, both sides ultimately win because it gives this otherwise point-less hobby a meaning.

Most of the ribbing between myself, Thomas and Terence mainly centred around United losing, which wasn't that uncommon back then. We couldn't really get into the nitty-gritty of derby game bragging rights because of a distinct lack of them. City were relegated from the old First Division in the 1986/87 season, and it took a couple of goes for them to bounce back up. So there was a two-and-a-half-year hiatus between Manchester derbies. By that time I was all in. I'd become obsessed with United and wanted to absorb any available information on the club. It was like I was making up for lost time. The thing is, this was an era before the internet, and even football as the all-pervading cultural phenomenon it is now. There were some live games on television but football didn't really enjoy mainstream coverage. *Match of the Day* lost the rights to league games in 1988 and didn't win them back until the start of the Premier League (although they did have the FA Cup), so most of my memories of watch-ing football at that time are on ITV, with *The Match* or

The Granada Match, and of course, the brilliant *Saint and Greavsie*.

With a lack of online resource and limited telly coverage, a big part of my football education came from one of my favourite places in the world – the library. For younger readers, libraries used to be everywhere before the government decided books were rubbish and stopped funding them. They were like an internet you could walk around, except there was less porn and the only cookies you could accept came in vending machines. My local library was at Abraham Moss, the local high school and leisure centre, and it was a place of learning and endless discovery. I used it for everything, from diving into the world of *Asterix the Gaul* to navigating my way around *Choose Your Own Adventure* books to listening to cassette tapes of Peter Cook and Dudley Moore and Spike Milligan. I'd go as far as to say that the library was the single biggest cultural influence of my formative years. I appreciate that may seem a bit pretentious in the age of tellies, but anything I saw on TV I wanted to read about at the library. And it wasn't cerebral stuff either. It was *Wizbit* and New Kids On The Block and football.

Once I got into football, a whole previously unexplored corner of the library opened up to me. I found a new home in the sports section and started making up for lost time. I feverishly consumed every page of the likes of *Manchester United: The Official History*, *Red Devils in Europe* and *Manchester United: A Complete Record 1878–1986*, as well as every old annual and yearbook going. The only major downside was that all of these football books happened to be big old hardbacks, so carrying them home was a nightmare. I got fitter reading about football than actually playing it. Former players I had no right knowing about were branded upon my brain forevermore. I learnt all about Billy Meredith (and the fact he used to play with a toothpick in his mouth), Jack 'The Gunner' Rowley (who played in an era when match reports came in the very cool form of cartoon strips) and the more contemporary 'Big' Jim Holton (who I discovered was 6 ft 2 in tall, had blue eyes and had a propensity to hunt people down). This intensive course in Manchester United also introduced me to the concept of adultery as I read about why Tommy Docherty ended up getting the sack.

Throughout this period, Thomas was always a reliable authority on the current situation at Old Trafford. I learnt about how United were spending a lot of money to try and compete with Liverpool and it wasn't really going as planned. Which was slightly confusing because the head-to-heads were very even affairs, with United probably having the better record during that period. I also got used to the common criticism that United were a 'one-man team' and that man was Bryan Robson. As good as he evidently was, my first footballing hero was Mark Hughes. He was like a superhero. Not only did he score spectacular goals, from net-busting volleys to gravity-defying overhead kicks, but his broad shoulders and muscular thighs meant he was built like a caped crusader too. Not to mention the fact he had the coolest nickname – I mean, 'Sparky'! I bloody loved him and thought he was the best player in the world. My all-encompassing fandom was further cemented by my older sister Usmaa. She was going through her own fast-track Red Devil conversion at high school, except fuelled by actual mates rather than books. I was still at the age where everything she was into was really cool and so the fact she supported United was the ultimate validation as her annoying copy-cat mini-me.

I soon realised that school jumble sales were a rich source of United-centric tat, much to my mum's consternation. I'd use all of my spends on collecting anything to do with the club. There were always old *Match* and *Shoot* annuals from the 1970s and early 1980s knocking about in and among the *Look-In* annuals and tatty Enid Blyton paperbacks. If you were really lucky, you'd stumble across a player figure or even a United-themed boot bag. I was gutted when my mum wouldn't let me buy some well-worn black Bryan Robson shinpads, even though they absolutely stank. Both my parents were vehemently against me wearing anything that was second-hand or 'pre-loved', because they saw it as undignified and almost an insult to them that I'd want something discarded by someone else – which I get, but it didn't stop them happily accepting hand-me-downs from friends and family. Maybe it's because they knew where they came from. But missing out on those shinpads was a blow. I remember Kevin Sadler, who I used to sit next to at dinner-time, brought in a late-1970s United top signed by all the players which he'd stolen from his older brother. Unfurling it onto our packed lunch table, he asked me if I wanted to buy it for a pound. I said thanks but no thanks – why would I want to spend such an extortionate amount on a football top with black felt-tip marks all over it? Idiot.

By the time we were in Junior 4 and therefore the top dogs at C-Wood (so we could finally sit on the benches at the back of assembly rather than cross-legged on the minging floor), City were back up in the top division. After three school years – a lifetime for a kid – we could finally look forward to a real-life Manchester derby. We were buzzing for it, as was the city as a whole. The *Manchester Evening News* were hyping it up, as were *North West Tonight*, GMR, *Piccadilly Gold* and *Granada Reports* with Elton Welsby. We were just a few months away from the end of the 1980s and less than a year away from big school. The future lay sparkling ahead, with the 1990s promising flying cars and Metal Mickeys in every home. Perhaps this first derby since what seemed like forever would give us some kind of indicator as to which of the Manchester clubs would enjoy the better decade to come. Terence was loving it, giving it the big 'un, even though he must have known deep down that United were strong favourites and the likely victors. Tom and I were quietly confident, even though Robson was out injured (again). We weren't any great shakes but we were better than a newly promoted City, surely. Terence was raving about Paul Lake and David White (who looked very handy in highlights ahead of the game) but they were no match for Sparky Hughes, Choccy McClair, Paul Ince et al. It was for this reason we were pretty sure Maine Road would witness a one-sided rout.

I am sure, if you've come into contact with any City fan of a certain age for any period of time in the last 30-odd years, you will know that we weren't wrong about the hiding, just about who was delivering it. It was a 5–1 humiliation, with David Oldfield (twice), Trevor Morley, Ian Bishop and Andy Hinchcliffe gleefully handing us our arses. Hughes got our goal, a typically gymnastic scissor-kick that deserved a much happier context, but really it was no kind of consolation. I was gutted. We lived just off the always busy Cheetham Hill Road, a main artery into the city centre or 'town', and that evening we could hear people celebrating and beeping horns. Presumably it was for City, but who knows, maybe Woolworths were giving away free cola cubes. The thing is, if we'd lost 5–1 to Liverpool it would still be horrible but you could kind of deal with it because Liverpool were so good. But we'd never been *thrashed* by Liverpool – not in my admittedly short lifetime anyway. It was always an odd goal or two either way. City – CITY!! – had beaten us 5–1. There was no way of justifying it or making sense of it in my head. Hinchcliffe's open-palmed five-fingered celebration for their last goal became an iconic reminder of that day for years to come. Terence was of course chuffed to bits and waved five gloating digits at us for days. He also wrote out the score (with scorers) repeatedly everywhere, and why not?

It was the first game that left me numb. They say the first cut is the deepest, and it's true. Granted Cat Stevens/ Yusuf Islam was referring to the break-up of a seminal relationship, but he could just as easily have been lamenting about getting walloped at Maine Road. The media reported on the lopsided scoreline as something far bigger than just some freak result. It was seen as symbolic of the expensive, dysfunctional Reds versus the dynamic, vibrant City. Through a combination of justified faith and practical necessity, City manager Mel Machin had promoted the best part of the club's FA Youth Cup winning side, their 'Class of '86'. Ian Brightwell, Steve Redmond, Paul Lake, Andy Hinchcliffe, David White and Jason Beckford had all come through together and their collective pride, energy and fearlessness was seen as fundamental to the win. We had a few young prospects at United, including Russell Beardsmore and Lee Sharpe, but could only dream of a similar 'Class of ...' scenario at Old Trafford. Fergie had made a big deal out of restructuring and revitalising the youth set-up at United but we were still waiting for the fruits of his revamp. Meanwhile he was spending big on underperforming players who would surely just block their progress anyway.

They say you don't choose who you support. Well, I did, but that's only because our family was brand new to the country and had no previous allegiance. But I was glad that I supported United, over City or Liverpool or Arsenal or anyone. For good or for bad, United quickly became a vital part of me; a part that was to grow and in many ways take over. And spoiler alert: it worked out quite well. However United's fortunes may peak and dip for the rest of my days, I am ever grateful that my childhood and then adolescent years coincided with the most glorious period in the club's history. Other parts of my life may have been a ball of confusion and contradiction and all those awkward questions of identity, but the three constants I was grateful for – football, family and my religion (not necessarily in that order) – remained my armbands and white float in the choppy Harpurhey swimming baths that is life. Sure there was the occasional black brick on the bottom of the pool that I had to dive down and recover, but nothing as tortured as this metaphor. Football – and United – are responsible for some of the best memories and closest friendships of my life. Alas sadly, I don't know what Thomas and Terence are doing now.

Speaking of memories, remember the man behind the wire? The scruffy fella I befriended in the playground who would lark about outside the Egerton? I was told in no uncertain terms to stop humouring him and stay away. Not by a teacher or dinner lady, but by an older girl. Turns out the actions he was performing and getting me to copy were monkey gestures. No wonder he was pissing himself as I innocently played along. I was the one acting like I was in Chester Zoo; a little brown kid dancing about for his idle amusement. So yeah, fuck that guy.

2.

NEVER MIND THE COSSACKS, HERE'S ANDREI

'And-rei Kan-chel-skis.' Even his name sounds musical and fittingly onomatopoeic for a player whose running style was all staccato movements and darting bursts. Although broad shouldered and deceptively strong, Andrei's game was much more about skips and rapid scampers than outmuscling the opposition. I'd love to regale you with something poetic about how he channelled Rudolf Nureyev on the wing, exhibiting all the elegant grace and balletic poise of a fleet-footed maestro, but that wasn't him either. In fact there was something quite neurotic and picky about his demeanour on the ball, like a nervous junkie avoiding dog turds in Piccadilly Gardens, albeit in an aesthetically pleasing way. There was something wonderfully idiosyncratic about the way he dribbled past defenders: he didn't have the silky slalom of a John Barnes raid, nor the lazy mulleted lollop of Chris

Waddle in full flow. Kanchelskis was so different. It probably makes no sense to describe him in this way, but to me he seemed to play in a foreign language.

I always felt a deep personal affinity with our Andrei. The sense that our lives converged and entwined for a brief but intoxicating period during the early 1990s. He, a precociously talented footballer from the USSR. Me, an asthmatic little Asian kid with a stutter and a dream. A Cold War-thawing foreign exchange programme that only one of us was aware of. Destiny's wind brought Andrei to Manchester, while I on the other hand, well, I stayed in Manchester too. But spiritually I was a stranger in Moscow, queuing up for stale loaves at the local bakery and swearing allegiance to the hammer and sickle with a Mancunian twang. Granted he was swapping Donetsk for Didsbury in a seismic shift in geography, language, custom, culture and prevailing economic system – and I was still at school in Cheetham Hill – but let's chalk it down to trying new things. And if it wasn't quite the momentous historic moment in global diplomacy that existed in my head, it was at least worthy of one of those Channel 4 life-swap shows: a small but noticeable twitch of the Iron Curtain. Famed world figures such as Reagan and Gorbachev may have grabbed the headlines, but Andrei's dribbles and my fingering surely deserve some mention in the footnotes of history.

If anything, I was a couple of years ahead of Andrei in terms of Anglo-Russian assimilation. While my Soviet soulmate was still establishing himself as a promising youngster at Dynamo Kyiv, I was playing a small but significant part in strengthening ties with the Russian Federation. There may have been two thousand miles between Crumpsall and the Kremlin, but Manchester always boasted long-held ties with the glorious Red Army (Soviet, not Stretford End) – dating back to when two rum German lads by the names of Fred Engels and Karl Marx started meeting at Chetham's Library to outline early plans for Communism with only Greggs pasties for sustenance. In my case, the instrument wasn't the means of production but an actual instrument. It all started during a Cravenwood assembly much like any other. We were casually told that Russian instruments would be taught at the school, courtesy of the occasional presence of a bearded chap in brown corduroys called Mr Hulme. Now, I was sceptical of new teachers at the best of times, never mind ones with links to foreign superpowers and questionable trousers. What exactly was his game?

My entire perception of the Russian people was based on Ivan Danko (Arnold Schwarzenegger) from *Red Heat*, as well as Ivan Drago (Dolph Lundgren) and Ludmilla Vobet Drago (Brigitte Nielsen) from *Rocky VI* – so an Austrian and two Scandinavians. They taught me that all Russians were scarily sexy, largely monotone, built like brick shithouses and adorned with perfectly angular blond flat-tops. It didn't much matter to me that Mr Hulme's hair was largely unkempt and mousy brown – a clever disguise to hide his cuboid barnet no doubt. All I knew was that he was one to watch. I may have even whispered as much to a nonplussed Azeem sitting cross-legged next to me. Funnily enough, I did a bit of reading up many years later and there was something of a breaking down barriers element to the whole thing. Of the many cities Manchester is twinned with around the world – including Faisalabad in Pakistan and Wuhan in China – one notable 'sister' municipality is Saint Petersburg (formerly Leningrad). It turns out the push to teach Russian musicianship to Mancunian youth was seen as a 'pioneering initiative' to strengthen cultural ties between the cities and to 'dispel many of the Cold War myths prevalent at the time'. It certainly worked for us.

A bit of soft diplomacy was no bad thing. It's easy to forget how closed off and otherworldly the Eastern Bloc in general and the USSR in particular felt before glasnost and demokratizatsiya. Prior to the fall of the Berlin Wall and the rise of Mikhail Gorbachev, anything east of Checkpoint Charlie was very much a riddle and as other-worldly as Nicholas Lyndhurst taking a stroll around the corner to war-time London in *Goodnight Sweetheart*. Being privy only to snippets of news reports, *Spitting Image* puppets and pop culture reference points, everything Soviet seemed suspicious and slightly dangerous. It was the drip-drip-drip effect of every baddie in every Hollywood film having a vaguely Muscovite accent – up until Muslims and Arabs became the identikit villains du jour. The Russian charm offensive, certainly the one I experienced, wasn't nefarious or duplicitous in its intentions. It was just normal people – teachers and artists and musicians – trying to bridge the divide. Looking back it could even be described as sweetly hopeful and sadly naïve, in the context of modern-day cyber warfare, polonium poisoning and unconscionable war crimes in Ukraine.

Any suspicions I may have harboured about Mr Hulme's ulterior motivations were quickly dispelled as he was introduced to a small group of us. He was softly spoken to the point of shyness, saintly patient in the face of a thousand random questions and exuded the gentle demeanour of a reluctant health-food shop owner. I was volunteered alongside Jonathan and Dipak to try out for what Mrs Overfield hoped would become Cravenwood's very own band of Russian players. This didn't surprise me one bit. Mrs Overfield had previous for pulling me out of the class to try out for various instruments. Bless her, she seemed convinced that I had some very well-hidden talent for music despite growing evidence to the contrary. First it was the recorder, then the violin (to follow in the tone-deaf screeching footsteps of my two older sisters) and most recently the trombone, which was the worst of the lot. It was cumbersome, left my lips chapped and raw, and I honestly couldn't get on with anything that had a 'spit valve'. Gross. But maybe pairing me with something more Rasputin than Glenn Miller was just crazy enough to work.

We were each handed a triangular-shaped guitar called a balalaika and told it was the national instrument of the USSR. Thankfully there was no spit valve to speak of, just an elegant neck leading to a sort of big wooden samosa. The way Mr Hulme took such great care in liberating the instruments from their leather cases and handing them to us one-by-one made it feel as if we were in receipt of something sacred. As a child with no frame of reference, you tend to faithfully place the same value in a particular object or artefact as an adult does. Mr Hulme made these strange wooden vessels seem like the most precious things in the world, and that's exactly how we received them. I went from disinterested to honoured in a beat. My sense of privileged wonderment only increased when Mr Hume spotted the way I was holding my instrument. I was the mirror image of my schoolmates, with my left arm cradling the angular body and my right hand clutching the neck. 'Ah, you're a leftie!' Mr Hulme remarked, no doubt pleased that he'd discovered a potential comrade at the same end of the political spectrum/plectrum. 'We'll get that restrung for you and it can be yours.' I was gobsmacked. At home I'd get bollocked for eating with my left hand and yet here my southpaw default was being encouraged.

We had 30 school minutes blocked off each week to convene with Mr Hulme and perfect our Soviet-style strumming. To be honest, the thrill of being allowed to leave the classroom on a secret mission (that everyone knew about) was more than worth it. There was also the surprising revelation that we didn't sound horrible. Mr Hulme's tutelage was calm and persevering, never getting visibly annoyed at our cack-handedness or short caffeine-addled attention spans. He didn't get particularly animated when we were doing something right either, but you could tell he was pleased by the hint of a smile that threatened to break through his face fuzz. The school must have been pleased with our progress too because the Russian cultural influence grew beyond just us jamming away. Before long we had a whole troupe of folk-style Russian dancers to accompany our increasingly melodic efforts. Thankfully I didn't go anywhere near the dance lessons, but my springy Zebedee-like younger brother Shaf was roped into that. He bloody loved it, as did his fellow performers, as they crossed and uncrossed their arms to our tune and jumped up and kicked out their feet sporadically like Phil Jones on speed. The Brothers Choudry weren't the only ones to get involved in the Cravenwood revolyutsiya.

Once we got to the stage where we were performance ready, both playing and dancing, we needed outfits to complete the whole Cossack vibe. The thing is, it wasn't like we could pop out to Top Man or Burton and grab ourselves a whole load of Doctor Zhivago-style kosovorotka shirts or baggy MC Hammer sharovary pants. I mean, baggy clothing *was* becoming the fashion of the day but Spliffy jeans didn't exactly scream Red Army (well not *that* one anyway). We needed bespoke alternatives and the teachers turned to that tried and tested failsafe option when school resources are stretched and needs are plenty – volunteer parents. A call was put out for help from amenable mums and dads, which sounds like a Batman-style signal was projected onto the overcast skies of North Manchester, but was more likely a letter home signed by headmaster Mr Dearing. And do you know who most readily answered that call for urgent assistance? Immigrant mums. No offence to parents of the Caucasian persuasion, of whom one or two always lent a hand, but it's mad how often the minority made up the majority when most needed, at least round our way. It was the same when jumble sales were being organised or food needed to be cooked for some reason or trips needed to be supervised – brown and black mums were always the ones selling us stuff, feeding us seasoned delicacies and making us hold hands with our partners.

The opposite was true for some reason when it came to harvest collection, when white parents were far more forthcoming with tins of beans, pineapple chunks, pasta, cereal and Tip Top cans. Maybe the non-white parents were slightly more flummoxed at the idea of giving away stuff from the cupboards they'd bought and needed to cook for us. I have the distinct memory of nabbing a few tins of something or other from the kitchen without my mum's knowledge, although she probably knew – mums *always* do.

A few mums (and it was always mums rather than dads) who knew their way around a sewing machine volunteered their scarce time and were tasked with adding decorative strips of jacquard ribbon to the trim of plain white shirts. Mainly around the collar, the first few buttons from the top, and the cuffs. I don't know if my mum was the best amateur tailor or the most gullible, but she was given the lion's share of the work. I was a combination of proud and then increasingly annoyed as I saw her slaving away for hours on the garments at the same time as looking after the five of us over-energetic kids. At least the school was effusively grateful for her efforts and that seemed to please her.

Everything was coming together nicely for a set of performances that the school and Mr Hulme were looking to organise. Vital to everything was obviously the quality of our playing (and prancing) and so preparations were ramped up. There was more practice time allotted to our musical sessions, and we were even allowed to take our balalaikas home for some extra-curricular honing of our skills. Goodness knows what the passers-by must have thought as I dawdled home with what looked like a Bugsy Malone splurge gun in tow. This musical lark was quickly taking over.

If all that sounds like hard work, it was a blessed relief from the other new aspect of my education that was the dreaded eleven-plus. The last couple of terms of Junior 3 and the summer holidays going into Junior 4 saw me cramming for exams I didn't really want to take. My parents were eager to try and get me into a local grammar, and they were encouraged by my Cravenwood teachers who were sure I was smart enough. I say my parents, it was more the case that my dad very much liked the idea of me going to grammar school but left all the actual preparation to my mum. I'd need to excel in the eleven-plus exams to have any chance of securing myself a place at one of these fancy schools. For everything they gave me in terms of encouragement, personal development, a happy environment and a real sense of belonging, Cravenwood had not prepared me for the specific skills and reasoning needed for grammar school entrance exams. It was like a game that I didn't know the rules for. I needed to learn, and fast. So bless my mum, with her limited English, zero knowledge of how to go about it, and an introverted shyness that belied her steely resolve to do anything to better her kids, she took it upon herself to get me match fit.

Looking back, I have so much respect for how she went about it. Remember these were the days before Google or even Ask Jeeves. My mum had no idea how she could help me pass those exams but that didn't stop her utilising everything and everyone that could help. In lieu of my dad's support (which would have been welcomed seeing as he had the means, the language, the contacts and the car to get out there and gather all the information she needed), she got my elder sisters Ayesha and Usmaa to fact find and research the best course of action. She also asked my primary school teachers for help and called upon family friends to explain things she didn't know. One of those friends was the mother of a boy who was my age and would be going in for the same exams at the same time. This proved something of a blessing because she could help with locating past papers, etc., and even kindly ferry me between tests along with her boy. Unfortunately for my mum, she didn't just have my dad's laissee-faire attitude to contend with in single-handedly getting me into a grammar school – she also had to deal with my mardy resistance to social mobility.

I didn't want to go to grammar school. For all the hopes and dreams my parents may have had for me to leave who we were and where we were in this new country and progress to a more refined echelon of society, it's not what I wanted. Don't get me wrong, it's not like I was some determined little communist or a working-class hero refusing to mix with toffs or even the petty bourgeoisie. I just didn't want to leave my mates. I was happy. Obviously I wanted to do well, have a good education and get a good job, but I was only 10 years old and more than anything I just wanted to go to a school where all my mates were going. That meant either Abraham Moss – where most Cravenwood alumni ended up – or the slightly more well-to-do Prestwich High. I'd always been top of the class at primary school and was pretty sure that would continue. There was only one thing for it – I had to have it out with them. So one day I sat them both down in the front room and told them in no uncertain terms that I could not and would not be a conduit for *their* ambitions; that I was an individual with my own agency and my own chosen fate to fulfil. Most importantly I told them that happiness is a far more noble aspiration than a fancy education or a well-paid job. And if you believe all that, you definitely didn't grow up in a first-generation immigrant household.

I was put to work revising for the entrance exams for Manchester Grammar, Bury Grammar, William Hulme Grammar (in Whalley Range) and Hulme Grammar (in Oldham). This involved test books on maths, science, English and 'reasoning'. As far as I could tell reasoning was like riddles, like 'A water flow is to a reservoir as a current is to a _____' or 'A football is to Andrei Kanchelskis as a balalaika is to a _____'. It was mostly fine because it was intuitive and I was good at stuff like that, but occasionally I'd come unstuck because the questions referenced words I'd not heard of, like 'pantry' or 'cul-de-sac' or 'marionette'. How the fuck was I supposed to know what I didn't know? That seemed unfair to me. It felt like a con to help the posh kids win. I was pretty good at the English stuff too, because I had a wild imagination and liked to write stories, although I'd sometimes get bored halfway through and start daydreaming or looking at the curtains and finding faces in them. But I really struggled with the maths and science stuff. No offence to the teachers at Cravenwood but the questions in the books were significantly more advanced than anything I'd been taught before. Plus my brain didn't work as well on numbers and decimals and how fast a car was going to reach its destination in one hour.

During the days and weeks and months of prepping, I didn't know why I was being punished – because that's what it felt like. As if I'd been bad and therefore had to work on sums and things instead of playing outside or watching TV or having any sort of fun. I didn't get why everyone was being extra strict with me specifically and making me sit in silence with a book and a pencil while I could hear my siblings messing about. The seriousness of school – and learning stuff – seemed to have suddenly gone from 0 to 100 out of nowhere, and the fear was it would be like this forever if I actually got into one of these schools. To this day I hate the idea of young kids having the stress of tests and revision and exams at an age when education should still be fun. The act of learning isn't intrinsically miserable. It needn't feel like a chore, especially when you're at an age when you're a willing sponge and every second thing you say is a question anyway. Of course I don't blame my parents for putting me through that arduous period of cramming, because they clearly felt that I was worth the effort and wanted the best for me. I just didn't know why I couldn't just go to a normal school like everyone else I knew and have a good education there instead.

Funnily enough, my first regular taste of a 'normal' high school came via Russian music. After weeks of honing our skills at Cravenwood, Jonathan, Dipak and myself were deemed good enough to take the next step. With parental permission, we were invited to join rehearsals for the grand-sounding Kalinka Youth Balalaika Orchestra, which convened at Trinity C of E High School in town on a weekly basis. Turns out Mr Hulme had been going into various schools in the area and plucking the best to join the Kalinka ensemble. I like to think we were the 1980s primary school version of the Class of '92 – a golden generation of precociously talented youngsters ready to wow and amaze that tiny slither of Mancunians who were really into Soviet folk songs. And no doubt somewhere in deepest darkest Siberia there was the Russian equivalent of Alan Hansen quietly seething. Jonathan's parents were kind enough to drop us off and pick us up each week as a whole new world opened up to me. The sessions were in the evening, which made them massively more exciting. Not only did we get to spend time in a high school, but it was an *empty* high school – and at night too. I always had this weird fantasy as a child of sleeping over at school, but in some ways this was even better because it was big school after dark. There could be no greater thrill – apart from maybe wandering around a closed Toys R Us, which remains an unfulfilled ambition.

The weekly Kalinka trips meant I was now familiar with the inner workings of two high schools – Trinity and

Abraham Moss (which I knew as a library, leisure centre, panto season theatre and nearby pitch to play football). Both were much bigger but largely similar looking to Cravenwood, in that they were built in the 1970s to early 1980s, had that generic boxy look and had similar reference points adorning the halls and walls. They also shared a vital characteristic that I didn't recognise until later and completely took for granted at the time: diversity. Not only was there a healthy mix of race and religion apparent among the intake at both Abraham Moss and Trinity, but just like Cravenwood they were 'mixed', i.e. not single sex. The transition from primary to secondary school is always a significant one; you go from being surrounded by infants and kids who can't tie their own laces to an environment that includes hairy six-foot-tall 15- and 16-year-olds who smoke and spit on the floor. It takes some getting used to and makes you grow up quickly from a standing start. That said, those early tastes of secondary life didn't cause me to worry about how I'd cope or fit in, especially if I had a bunch of mates going through the same thing alongside me.

The experience of attending entrance exams was a whole different matter. There was so much I didn't recognise, and it was nearly all extremely foreboding. Everything felt so grown up and serious. I don't even mean 'teenage' grown up or 'spitting on the ground' grown up – I mean adult, smoking a pipe not a cigarette grown up. The worst in that respect was Manchester Grammar School, which to me felt like an actual university. It was so huge and grand; everything was so austere and old-fashioned. It honestly felt like the setting for *Chariots of Fire* or what I'd seen on the news of the Houses of Parliament. Weirdly for my age, I loved listening to *The Goon Show* (from cassette tapes I borrowed from the library) and they always made fun of old-fashioned authority figures from the 1950s. This lot felt like that. I'm sure it wasn't quite as grand as it felt, and the teachers I thought were 100 years old were probably just in their mid-40s. But at that age I had no reference point for what I was experiencing. From the outside it was like a massive stately home, and inside everything was old, dusty and made of dark wood. I'd see lists upon lists of names etched in gold on the walls. Not names I knew like Usman or Dale or Kevin, but Bernhard and Godfrey and Samuel. There was no chance in hell you'd ever see a Nooruddean up there.

What made it harder – at all of the entrance exams for each of the grammar schools – is that the other boys all seemed to know each other. They'd be chatting away in their little cliques like old friends and would look at me and snigger among themselves (possibly because I was gawping at them, in fairness). It's how I imagined that I'd be with my mates if this was Abraham Moss or Trinity High and one of these posh lads was there, doing humanitarian work or something. They were nearly all white and obviously all boys, which is how it dawned on me that these were single-sex schools. Every little thing made me feel different to everyone else: from the clothes (a lot of the boys were wearing suits or smart uniforms, presumably from their fee-paying junior schools that fed into these fee-paying secondary schools) and even the basic stationery we were each holding. They seemed to have all the gear, neatly packed away in cases, sets and compartments. I had a see-through polythene bag with two pens (in case one ran out), a pencil and a ruler. Also I was definitely the only lad wearing any form of velcro fastening, while my heavily padded cream-coloured jacket made me look like a little Asian Stay-Puft Marshmallow Man.

Looking back I should have really freaked them out by wearing my favourite Lenin badge, courtesy of celebrated balalaika soloist Mikhail Danilov of the Rimsky-Korsakov State Conservatory. He visited Manchester from our twinned city of Leningrad to perform with us at the Royal Northern College of Music, which was by far our biggest concert yet. By now we were a legit little orchestra, with prima balalaikas, alto balalaikas, bass balalaikas (similar to ours but massive, like genetically modified mutant samosas), domras (like balalaikas but rounded rather than triangular, they reminded me of the instrument the rooster played in Disney's *Robin Hood*), the occasional gusli (like a Russian zither), the even more occasional svistulka (a squeaky-sounding little whistle that made middle-class audiences laugh), a horn called a zhaleika that sounded like a wistful goose, and Russian spoons, which were every bit as basic an instrument as they sound. When you combine all that with our Cossack dancers, we were able to put on quite a show. The fact that Danilov could join us for a one-off special performance was the cherry on top of the korolevsky torte.

Danilov brought with him a number of other notable performers from his Conservatory (which sounds less impressive if your first thought like me is a glass extension with wicker furniture). One was a kindly-looking veteran gusli player who was clearly held in high regard; to my shame I don't recall his name. There were other balalaika players too who were slightly older and far superior to us. They were clearly doing the heavy lifting when it came to the concert, but we held our own. I stood out because a) Dipak and I were the only brownies, and b) I was the one leftie who ruined the aesthetic (and probably drove the OCD-ers in the audience to distraction). The performance was by all accounts a triumph and everyone was in jubilant mood afterwards. We were introduced to various notable dignitaries and invited guests who were effusive and very kind in their praise. I wasn't really interested in council officials and their like until we got to a chap named George Scanlon, who we were told worked with Manchester United and other football clubs – he was only Andrei Kanchelskis's translator! I was too shy to ask him anything about his day job but I wondered then as I wonder now whether he happened to bring along any work friends with a propensity to tiptoe past defenders and cut in from the right.

Backstage we gathered around Danilov and the kindly gusli player for autographs (I'm not sure why, but I wanted one because everyone else wanted one). This was obviously a normal thing for both of them because they had pre-printed picture cards to sign. As well as this, Danilov was also kind enough to gift each of us with gold enamel pins decorated with a deep-red plastic lacquer. Mine showed Vladimir Lenin in heroic pose with what I assumed was his golden signature underneath. It was stunningly beautiful and became a prized possession. So much so that I took to wearing it at every opportunity – in school, out of school, everywhere. It must have raised a few eyebrows at the local Kwik Save – a little Pakistani boy swanning about Cheetham Hill wearing blatant communist propaganda on his lapel while looking for Findus Crispy Pancakes in the frozen food aisle. These were the days before Al-Qaeda when any connection with Russia was seen as far scarier than a Muslim wearing a backpack.

As much as these well-intentioned 'hands across the divide' initiatives are often lampooned for being hollow gestures with little or no real-world impact, they can and often do make a massive difference at a community level. It's really easy, not to mention mean-spirited, to be cynical and dismiss them as idealistic nonsense organised by deluded hippies. But those same hippies are far more effective at dispelling a fear of the 'other' and bringing people together in a constructive way than the kind of politicking that frames any form of diplomacy. I certainly know that no one involved in Kalinka or any of our very amateur musical misadventures was afraid of Russian people or Russian culture by the end of it. Rather we embraced it because it was fun and different and that difference wasn't a scary thing. There were times when I wished that I'd learnt to play the guitar instead – partly because it's very rare that you're at a party and happen across a balalaika to play and impress everyone – but I learnt to appreciate that what we were doing was special and unique in a good way.

My love for Russian culture was obviously bolstered by the fact that my favourite player at the time belonged to that culture – even though Kanchelskis was born in Ukraine with Lithuanian heritage, and due to the rapidly changing geopolitical landscape of the time represented three different national teams in the Soviet Union, CIS (Commonwealth of Independent States) and Russia. Regardless, to me he was always our Russian on the wing. He is one of those players who is far more fondly remembered and highly rated by United fans than anyone else (barring Everton supporters and maybe Rangers too). The mere mention of his name makes fans of a certain vintage smile and go all misty-eyed. In some ways, he was the proto-Cristiano Ronaldo. Skilful and twinkle-toed, but always preferring to take the more direct route to goal with his powerful running and deceptive strength. A major difference is however that he didn't quite fulfil his potential, which is sad but also much more romantic in that shoulda-woulda-coulda kinda way. There were various issues he had to contend with, from shadowy figures in his entourage (one of whom tried to hand Fergie an unexplained and swiftly rejected £40,000 'gift', according to SAF's autobiography), Lee Sharpe constantly vying for his position and the daft foreigner rule in Europe which meant he was regularly omitted from the Champions League squad.

Still, he did win two Premier League titles, one FA Cup, one League Cup, a European Super Cup and millions of hearts while at Old Trafford, so it wasn't all bad. Year on year, Kanchelskis bagged more and more goals during his United career, which peaked in the first half of the 1994/95 season, his last at the club, when he was scoring for fun. It was during this purple patch that we finally got revenge for the 5–1 derby defeat in '89 by thrashing City 5–0. Kanchelskis set up Eric Cantona for the opener with a gorgeous lofted through-ball and before scoring a hat-trick himself. It was his defining game in a defining season, which ended with him being awarded the fans' Player of the Year. And then he left. Amid confusion, claim and counter-claim, he was sold to Everton in a cloudy transfer with a cloudier transfer fee. Shakhtar were owed a big percentage of any resale value, allegedly waived it and then angrily demanded it, claiming they were duped by Andrei's agent. We didn't give a shit about any of that. All we knew was that we'd lost our boy. It made no sense. Something great just sort of … fizzled out.

My budding balalaika career, such as it was, went the same way. Things were going great, we were enjoying performing and there was even the opportunity of possibly performing abroad – a trip to Russia was mooted. But it was getting in the way of school and was taking up too much time so I dropped out. Again, it's a case of what could have been. Worse news than my balalaika hopes being kiboshed, or even Andrei leaving United, was to follow. Among the various letters back from grammar schools was one from Bury. I'd got in. Goodbye Abraham Moss. Goodbye Prestwich High. Goodbye mates. My only consolation was I'd not got into the even posher Manchester, where I'd passed my first exam and been invited to a second. I even got a further interview with them – a music interview. The teacher in charge was fascinated by my balalaika playing and asked me all sorts of questions about Russian music. He reeled off a few Russian composers and asked me who my favourite was. By way of a nervous joke I blurted out 'Andrei Kanchelskis', but he wasn't amused. So it was *dasvidaniya* (goodbye) to that and a toddle back to Crumpsall with giant samosa in tow.

3.

NORMAN WHITESIDE ZINDABAD!

To this day I don't understand the logic or how it came about. Going into town ('town' being the city centre of Manchester and more specifically the Arndale Centre) was a big deal for us at that age. We'd need a bloody good reason, with the strict proviso of heading straight back home once we were done. Bussing it to Old Trafford unaccompanied was out of the question. And on an actual match day? Fuhgeddaboudit. If we'd ever raised such a foolish notion as a gang of us popping down to Alton Towers for a day of merriment and candy floss, we'd have been laughed out of the house – before being told off for being out of the house. Exasperated laments on our part that our white friends were allowed to get away with this, that and the other with impunity were greeted with the bitterly sarcastic suggestion that we should perhaps go and live with them, if that was our idea of paradise (to which the unspoken response was always 'if only ...').

Our parents were dead strict but not uniquely so. As with other first-generation immigrants at the time, they were highly risk-averse on their children's behalf and certainly wouldn't stand for any backchat to the contrary. After all, beyond that front door was a world full of untold dangers, cruel prejudices and any number of Godless deviants. Which begs the question: why in the name of all that is halal would they send two of us to Pakistan on our own?

I was 11 and barely out of primary school; my sister Ayesha was the grand old age of 16 by just a couple of weeks. Together we were deemed responsible and old enough to make the 3,800-mile trip to the other side of the world. But of course we would be driven down to Heathrow Airport with the whole family first (with at least three of us sitting on each other's laps) because *that* would be dangerous. The funny thing is, if we were heading down to London for any other reason, we'd have been beyond excited and it would have been a proper treat. Instead we were various levels of stressed, nervous, confused and petrified. It wasn't just our respective tender ages and the lack of parental chaperone that was odd/mad. Ayesha and I also happened to be the two most introverted and shy of the five of us Choudry children. Usmaa, Shaf and even little Saadia were far more outgoing and gregarious. Ayesha may have been the eldest, but she was quiet and studious and kind-hearted and gentle. There are old 16-year-olds and young 16-year-olds, and Ayesha was definitely the latter. I wasn't as innately good as her but I was still painfully shy around people I didn't know. Together we were a veritable tag team of keeping our heads down and hoping people left us alone. The point is, as mad as it was to send two children on this epic journey to a far-flung foreign land on their own, it was madder still to pick the two of us.

The whole thing was my dad's doing. My mum was just as nervous and concerned as the madcap plan duly warranted. Why couldn't one of our parents go with us? If that wasn't an option due to cost or circumstance or whatever then why did we need to go at all? Were we heading to a lavish wedding? No. Was there urgent business to attend to that only two young kids had the unique ability to negotiate? No. Was there, Allah forbid, a gravely ill relative whose last wish was specifically to see the two of us (but definitely not one of the other three)? Thankfully no. There seemed to be no rhyme or reason to the whole escapade; the only thinking being 'just because'. Racking my brains now, I can only assume that my dad had come to the sudden conclusion that me and my sister needed easing out of our shells and this was his rather extreme crab mallet solution. Either that or he had much more faith in us than we had in ourselves.

The risks weren't just isolated to the pair of us getting lost somewhere along the way, or taking a wrong turn in a foreign airport with only a rudimentary grasp of the language. The flight was due to stop in the Middle East before continuing on to Pakistan. I don't know if you've heard of him but there was a fella called Saddam Hussein who was causing a bit of a ruckus at the time. I'll try and explain it as succinctly as I can using my very basic understanding of the situation back then. Apparently he'd had a right old scrap with Iran that lasted nearly a decade and cost loads of money. By the time the scrap was over, he owed all that money to Kuwait who he'd borrowed it off. Kuwait was dead rich (because of oil) but kind of small and not very hard. Definitely not the cock of the region. So Saddam thought, forget paying them back, I'll just threaten them with an invasion (using weapons he'd bought with the money he'd borrowed off them). The USA got wind of this and were like, no one invades other countries for oil apart from us, and so told Saddam don't you dare otherwise we'll come over there with our mates (the UK, France, etc.) and sort you out. Anyway, that's basically how things stood when our flight was due to stop slap bang in the middle of everything. And by the 'middle', I mean Kuwait International Airport – where the US Marine Corps fought the biggest tank battle in its history.

Thankfully that didn't happen on our way to Pakistan, although the situation was precarious enough to put our refuelling stop at risk. Before all that it was goodbye to everyone at Heathrow. I was inconsolable. I'd never spent more than a couple of days away from my mum and dad and here we were on our way to the motherland for a whole six weeks. My poor sister did her best to console me but she must have been just as petrified about what lay ahead. She was so young to be tasked with not only looking after herself but also a hysterical little kid. If anything had happened to me – if I'd have wandered off as she momentarily turned her head or disappeared while she'd popped to the loo – it would have been on her. An intelligent but naïve 16-year-old who should have been busy with a *Look-in* magazine at home, not a teary-eyed 11-year-old at departures. Once on the plane, I was still sad and confused but such emotions had taken a back seat to genuine intrigue. We didn't go on holidays when I was a kid. I'd been to Pakistan once before when I was far too young to remember anything. Going 'back home' to visit relatives was rare, but going abroad for the sole purpose of 'relaxing' or 'having fun'? It was pure *baqwaas* (nonsense).

There's three things I specifically recall about the flight: earphones, turbulence and orange juice. Despite the long-haul aspect of the journey, there was no TV or video facilities to keep us occupied. I was given a colouring set and crayons, which felt like some kind of sick joke. I was young but not that bloody young. One facility available to us was a pair of beige plasticky earphones, with a variety of radio stations to choose from. Considering the fact we shared and argued over a single Walkman at home, this was the height of luxury. It was only topped by the discovery that the orange juice was free. The first time the air hostess came over and asked if we wanted a soft drink or some juice, I looked to my sister to see if it was okay (assuming she was coughing up for it from some sort of allowance she'd been given from my dad). When Ayesha explained it was free, I was like yes please and keep them coming. Eventually I realised that you *can* have too much of a good thing: I started to feel ill after one too many fill-ups as the potassium started to hit. This wasn't helped by the aforementioned turbulence. It was the first time I'd experienced anything like it and it freaked me out then as it does now. There's nothing like rattling about in a giant metal tube and sporadically losing and gaining altitude to remind you that humans were never meant to be so high up. Again I looked to my sister for reassurance and was met with only a mirror of my own terror. I was so relieved when we enjoyed momentary respite on Kuwaiti terra firma for refuelling – even if that terra firma was coveted by neighbouring dictators. Better to die in a strange land than in mid-air.

Turbulence aside, we continued on our mostly smooth journey to the subcontinent. Although there was an unwelcome bump ahead. We were due to land in Karachi's Jinnah International Airport before transferring to a connecting flight to Lahore. Except due to a longer than planned stop in Kuwait, we missed the connection. So there was a long wait in a small, foreboding room in Karachi as they decided what to do with us. We were in a foreign country, thousands of miles away from our family and hundreds of miles away from any relatives. We were tired, jet lagged and at least one of us was uncomfortably full of orange juice. These were the days before mobile phones so we couldn't even let anyone know where we were or ask them what to do. All we could do was wait and hope that they'd find us two seats on a flight to Lahore. Just to add to our mild panic and major displacement issues, we were told there was an issue with our luggage. In an ongoing effort to advance the next generation of Pakistanis through the power of BBC Acorns, my dad had included two computers (and accompanying floppy drives and educational disks) in giant suitcases for our paternal cousins. He had stressed to us – and by 'us' I mean my sister – that he had double-checked and triple-checked with the Pakistani consulate, as well as all the relevant authorities in both countries, that their transportation would be waved through without issue. Well, somebody was clearly lying because there was very much an issue.

Apparently no one from the consulate had spoken to the large moustachioed man who'd entered the room shortly after his pungent body odour did. After unpacking everything and forcefully trying to switch on machines that remained unplugged (including pressing hard and long upon the printed logo of an owl), he started asking questions about what they were for. My sister explained they were an educational tool for our young cousins, but this did little to assuage his curiosity. After popping out of one of those entrance heaters at shops when you come in from the cold, except the inside was outside and vice versa. The air was hot and dry and felt hard to swallow. It took me a moment to realise that the relatively cool airport was a fabricated oasis and the fan-assisted oven outside was the normal Pakistani climate.

The other thing I noticed was the same brightness that I'd seen a teaser of in Kuwait. It was like someone had been messing with the TV settings and everything was that little bit too washed out for your eyes. All the men were wearing white or off-white shalwar kameez; the women were draped in light colours too but more colourful. This sounds especially dumb even for a kid, but something else that took my eyes some significant time to adjust to was the amount of Pakistani people in Pakistan. It's not like I was expecting to walk out to a load of white people or a local Chinatown – logically I knew Pakistan would be full of brown people just like us – but I'd never been somewhere without *any* white people. Not a single Caucasian face to be seen. The airport security? Brown. The police officers? Brown. The well-to-do tourists? Brown. The people on advertising billboards? Brown (albeit a noticeably lighter shade). The taxi drivers? Brown (although that wasn't too dissimilar to Manchester). If you've grown up your whole life as a minority in the place you call home – to the extent that you always notice people who are the same as you and even get a buzz if they're on telly or have a good job – the novel experience of walking around an environment where *everyone* looks like you is a revelation. It's a nice feeling but it's also weird. As a second-generation immigrant who has only known Crumpsall and the surrounding areas, it's not as if you suddenly feel like you belong here, but that at least a *part* of you belongs. And it's an important, vital part.

We eventually arrived at the family home in Sahiwal to a warm welcome. Our paternal grandparents gave us a long warm hug and felt incredibly familiar, in spite of the distance there had been between us. We called our grandfather abu-ji and our grandmother ammi-jaan, which are versions of dad and mum but that's how it often works in multi-generational households. Grandchildren and marital additions to the family adopt the same names that everyone calls the oldest patriarch/matriarch figures. Apparently when I was born, they were both over visiting in Manchester and my ammi-jaan doted over me. Of course I didn't remember that but all of our grandparents, including nani-ami (my mum's mum) and nana-abu (my mum's late dad), felt like constants in our lives. I'd be drawing a picture and be told my grandfather would hold his pen like that; my sister would laugh at something and be informed that her smile was not her own, but instead an inheritance from her grandmother. There were also our parents' semi-regular international calls that would end with an awkward few minutes where we'd be summoned over to speak briefly to our grandparents. Our bad mix of Urdu and Punjabi would make a garbled sort of sense, enough to express a genuine and mutual love. To see them for real, rather than in photo albums or old home videos, was something beautiful.

The biggest thing I missed – apart from my family – was of course football. These days I'm amazed at how knowledgeable Pakistani and Indian fans are about the sport in general and their favourite clubs in particular, but back then, in Sahiwal at least, no one was remotely interested. It was cricket, hockey, squash and kabaddi in that order. Even carrom (a ridiculously addictive table-top game that's a sort of cross between pool and air hockey) ranked higher. If you mentioned football to anyone, their only real point of reference was that nearly all the footballs in the world were sewn in Pakistan. Thankfully there was the BBC World Service so I'd catch the odd football report on the radio, but that was it. I was gutted because my obsession for the game was just starting to bubble over. It was just a month or so since United had won the FA Cup against Crystal Palace, courtesy of a Lee Martin winner in the replay. The first game against Palace and the two semi-final games with Oldham had been classics. It was the cup campaign that allegedly saved Fergie's job, and a lot was being made of the emergence of Mark Robins. *Match* magazine had an article about him headlined 'Robinsmania', and there were even some comparisons to Gary Lineker. But the English striker who really caught the eye in the cup final was a super sub called Ian Wright. Whatever happened to him?

I still had fresh memories of Lineker and co. starring in the 1990 World Cup, which had cast an everlasting spell on me. I have never massively cared for the England football team. At most, I've sporadically wanted them to do well (most recently Gareth Southgate's team, mainly because they seem such a decent collection of individuals). But that World Cup in Italy was beguiling. It caught my imagination even more than United winning their first trophy since 1985. I think every young football fan must fall in love with their first proper World Cup. That's why arguments about the best one are so redundant. It all depends on who you are, where you're from, how old you were and what was happening in your life. For me, Italia '90 was seminal. I fell in love with players like Roberto Baggio, Roger Milla, Claudio Caniggia, Paul Gascoigne and Toto Schillaci. I became obsessed with Diego Maradona, and thought he *must* be the best player ever purely from his warm-ups. That World Cup for me was similar to how people describe going to see *Star Wars* for the first time. It opened up a new world – the storylines, the characters, the drama, the colours, the joy, the heartbreak – and I was hooked forevermore.

Meanwhile, here in Pakistan, I was living in a parallel universe where football never existed. My boy cousins and their pals all played cricket for hours in heat you could fry akoori eggs in, and I happily slow-cooked in the outfield. Cricket was a sport I'd always enjoyed without playing very often. Why would you when you could just play football instead? On the rare occasions we did organise a game of cricket, it was always with a bunch of Asian mates, either on the Abraham Moss playground during holidays or the car park behind Shopping Giant on Sundays. Much like the games in Pakistan, the rules were improvised. If you hit the wall without bouncing it was a six; if it bounced it was a four. Sometimes, when there weren't enough of us for a proper game, we'd place the plastic newsagent-bought wickets in front of a wall. If you edged the ball onto the wall behind you, you were out. At least in Pakistan there was no shortage of space and so we had a hand (stick) drawn boundary. There were also actual wickets we could twist into the ground and a real corky ball (which we'd substitute for a tennis ball in Manchester for fear of hitting a nearby car, or distant window if you were channelling Viv Richards). Unlike our asphalt games, which would attract a mixed bunch, everyone in Pakistan was *really* good – if a little casual in the sweltering outfield. I was as enthusiastic as anything but alas not very good, although everyone was incredibly patient and encouraging.

One day I bought a football from the bazaar (probably paying 10 times the standard price because they saw a mug coming). It was one of those generic clipart-style balls, white with black patches, but at least it was a casey instead of a flyaway. I convinced my new friends that we should have a game of football instead of the standard cricket, and they were right up for it. After some time persuading them that we should pick actual teams instead of just playing, we were off. The longer we played, the more kids joined in. It was great fun and we started to play football pretty much every day.

I still missed United though. There was no chatting to mates or reading *Match* and *Shoot* cover to cover. And sadly there was no Pakistani version of *Saint and Greavsie* on telly, although that would have been great. Television was rationed full stop. I don't recall how many channels were available but there can't have been many. The only member of the household who'd pay much attention to it on a regular basis was Uncle Raffique, who would sit down in front of the small screen and intently scour through lists of names that would appear on the news. At first I wondered whether he was looking at starting line-ups of some sort, maybe cricket teams. But it quickly became apparent it wasn't a fun activity, but rather a tense do-not-disturb ritual. It turns out it was lists of names of Pakistani nationals who had managed to safely flee from Kuwait, either back to Pakistan or to 'safe' countries nearby. Things had escalated quickly in the region and there was a big expat community over there. Uncle Raffique was specifically searching for his friends Sarwar and Anwar, who were also old pals of my dad. Thankfully they both made it out.

One day, Yasser, the youngest of the cousins we were staying with, excitedly came in with a newspaper and told me he'd found a game of football on TV. I wondered whether he'd got it wrong as we were still in the close season. Maybe it was an international or even a random friendly game. The listing just said 'FOOTBALL' next to a scheduled time. Even if it was a local five-a-side kick-about, I was in. When it aired I couldn't believe my luck. It was the 1985 FA Cup Final: Manchester United v Everton! I'd been feverishly swotting up on anything and everything to do with United's history so had read all about that final but never actually seen it. The only way of doing so back then was buying a commemorative VHS of the game. So for it to be showing in Pakistan felt like some sort of miracle. It was great seeing all the names and moments I'd read about come to life. Peter Reid's deflected shot hitting the post; Kevin Moran scything down Reid to become the first player to be sent off in the cup final; and of course, Norman Whiteside's glorious extra-time winner.

I continued to keep an eye out for any further football listings on TV, and sure enough there it was a week later. I couldn't wait to see who was playing this time. Another Cup Final maybe. Or perhaps they'd show an international game to mix things up. The Hand of God game even. As I settled down to get another dose of the beautiful game I discovered it was ... Manchester United v Everton in the 1985 FA Cup Final. So undeterred I watched it again. And the next week ... it was on again. And I watched it again. I don't know why or how that particular match became a weekly fixture on Pakistani telly, but I was into it. Whether through pure repetition, the traffic situation over there is unique for all sorts of reasons. There's a sort of organised chaos going on that is terrifying to an unaccustomed tourist but by some miracle seems to work. Amid the hustle and bustle, expensive cars share the roads with horse-drawn tanga carriages (which I absolutely adored and dearly hope is still a thing in Pakistani towns and cities) and battery-powered rickshaws. The rickshaws are colourful but they're nothing compared to Pakistan's world-famous truck art. Forget *Pimp My Ride*, this is Michelangelo My Motor, as the most colourful, ornate, hypnotic designs adorn what would otherwise be pretty standard mid-size trucks or buses. Indeed, such is the one-upmanship of these art installations on wheels that some have extensions and structural additions for extra decorating. Nothing I say here could do them justice. The intricate artwork, sweeping calligraphy, witty slogans and bells and whistles are a testament to the creativity of the Pakistani people – and their propensity for peacocking and showing off with such flair.

Undoubtedly the most terrifying and dumbest thing we did in Pakistan was take part in motorcycle races around local dust roads and alleyways with our cousins Usama and Mateen. We'd sit on the back as passengers, gripping tightly because our lives literally depended on it, as our fearless boy-racers would test the absolute limits of their loudly revving Honda Heroes. None of us were wearing helmets or any protective equipment, and so at the speeds we were going at, any knock or bump or skid could have proved fatal. Forget our relatively risk-averse parents in Manchester, even the adults in Pakistan would warn us against doing something so incredibly stupid. But the adrenaline rush was unreal. What made it even more exciting/unbelievably empty-headed was that our cousins were stupidly young – as in 12 and 13 years old. They were literal kids zipping about and taking turns like it was a tropical Isle of Man. Along with the football and cricket and weekly dose of Norman Whiteside, you can see why I was getting used to our new dwellings. It was a slightly different experience for my sister, though. She was a bit older and much more mature than all of us boys and there weren't really any girls of her age about. A lot of her days were spent on the chath (flat roof), reading or people watching or looking down on us having a kickabout. Her lot improved greatly when we went to stay with my mum's family in nearby Arifwala.

Things were a little more chilled out in Arifwala, mainly because there were fewer adolescent boys running amok. And my sister suddenly had people around her age and on her wavelength to hang out with. There was Fayyaz mamu, who was only four years older than her and possibly the nicest, kindest person I've ever met. Sadly he's no longer with us but he was always my favourite uncle and remains the template for how I try to treat my own nieces and nephews now. And there was Shada khala, our fun-loving youngest aunt who had her own beauty salon as part of the house. She got on with Ayesha like a house on fire. Although I was without my similarly aged boy cousins – the likes of Usama, Mateen, Haris and Yasser – I still enjoyed Arifwala for different reasons. No disrespect to Sahiwal, but I felt more of my mum's presence and her warmth in Arifwala – and a big part of that was her mother, my Nani-ami. She was basically a carbon copy of my mum but with white hair – from the way she looked to the way she spoke to her gentle nature – and she at once made me feel both at home and incredibly homesick. Again, she's no longer with us and I still miss her to this day.

One thing I had to get used to was my first real experience of living with – or even really meeting – someone with a mental disability. My Uncle Zaffar, who everyone affectionately called 'Pappu', was pretty severely mentally disabled. He couldn't speak beyond making noises that sounded aggressive but everyone seemed to understand, and he had the mental age of a young child. I was immediately afraid of him. I'd not encountered anyone like him, and so when I'd hear him shouting for help or getting frustrated or even moving in a way that I didn't understand to be 'normal', it freaked me out. Of course I'm embarrassed about that now, but it was all new to me. Everyone, especially Nani-ami, told me not to worry and about how sweet-natured Pappu was, but it took some time for me to realise that. But eventually I did.

Sometimes he did get upset, like when he dropped his favourite toy, or he could smell that tea was being made and no one had yet brought him some, or when he was anxious about where his mother was, but he was such a gentle soul. He was lovely with kids and one of the things that totally disarmed me was the way my Auntie Rashda would place her baby Shoab beside him, because Pappu's presence calmed him. Soon Pappu got used to me and would trust me to be around him and even hug him tenderly. He wasn't scary at all; he was loving and hugely loved, and clearly a blessing to the family. When it was time to leave Arifwala to return to Sahiwal, I was excited to get back to playing football and racing around on motorbikes again, but it was so hard to say goodbye to everyone in Arifwala. I'm glad that I didn't know then that it would be the very last time I'd ever see Nani-ami or Pappu or my young, fun-loving Uncle Fayyaz. These amazing people with a deep and instant love for you finally come into your life and then they're gone forever. It still makes me teary thinking about it now. What I'd give to revisit the Pakistan I remember and for each of them to still be there so I could give them the biggest hug. Bless them all.

Before long it was time to say goodbye to Sahiwal too. It was that time in my life when six weeks felt like two years, and as much as I was looking forward to getting back home to everyone in Manchester with all my heart, it was still a wrench to leave this new part of my family that I'd only just got to know. We'd always been alone in Manchester – me, my brother, my three sisters and my mum and dad. There were no uncles or aunties or grand-parents or anything. I used to get jealous when Asian mates would complain about huge extended families living close by (usually because it meant they couldn't do anything without it being reported back to their parents) because I thought they were so lucky. Our family in this country began with my parents and ended with us. As much as I still think it was bonkers that my dad sent two young kids to Pakistan on their own, I also think it was a gift. It broadened my world, helped me gain a better understanding of who I was and where we came from, and it gave me new people to love and be loved by. Perhaps most importantly, it made me proud to be Pakistani. So maybe my dad's daft idea wasn't so daft after all.

Top 5 pretend Asian uncles when I was growing up

5) David Attenborough: My dad absolutely adored David Attenborough. Most of our VHS collection was made up of recordings of the *Natural World* and *Wildlife on One*. If we wanted to tape something off the telly, there were certain videos we could record over but *never* an Attenborough one. He was a constant in my childhood, and although I was fond of him, sometimes he'd overstay his welcome when I wanted to watch something else. So *just* like a real uncle ...

4) Richard Briers: Whether it was playfully winding up Margot in *The Good Life* or getting increasingly flustered in *Ever Decreasing Circles*, Briers always had such a sweet, gentle aura about him. Not only that, but there was a childlike mischief to him which was massively appealing as a little kid. The only times he didn't feel like a cheery uncle was when he was being extremely serious in one of Kenneth Branagh's Shakespeare adaptations. That's when I realised he was actually acting.

3) Michael Parkinson: Everyone seems to remember Parky as the genial, friendly host of his hugely popular chat shows and there was definitely a big element of that. But even as a kid, I could see the Yorkshire in him. There was a no-nonsense gruffness just beneath the wrinkly surface that I quite liked. Even when he was playing along with Rod Hull and Emu, you could sense he was thinking: 'Okay, that's enough now, you little feathery bastard.' That said, I don't think I ever trusted him again after *Ghostwatch* and 'Mr Pipes'.

2) Trevor McDonald: The absolute don. I think for perhaps the entirety of his broadcasting career Trevor McDonald must have been one of the most respected, comforting and reassuring figures in the nation's collective consciousness. For someone who was predominantly known for relaying the news in a very straightforward, factual manner, he somehow managed to convey an authority and warmth that is hard to pinpoint or explain. Even us kids who were mostly allergic to the news looked forward to his wry little 'And finally …' cues for a slightly amusing story about a sweary parrot in Bury St Edmunds.

1) Bill Cosby: I'm sorry but it's true. As a kid he was the dream uncle. *The Cosby Show* was such a big deal at the time and in lieu of an Asian version we latched onto this successful, happy, educated and most of all loving ideal of a non-white family. At its head was Cliff Huxtable, our generation's Atticus Finch, but with a sense of humour. He was funny, kind, wise and the archetype of what you wanted a dad/uncle to be. It was crushing to realise I'd been wrong all along.

4.

IF IT WASN'T FOR THOSE PÉCSI MUNKÁS

My first day at Bury Grammar School for Boys wasn't long after I'd got back from Pakistan. This is pertinent for a few reasons. Firstly, and most weirdly, I came back with a different voice. I don't mean my voice had dropped; I was still as squeaky and nasal as ever. I mean my actual accent had changed. Instead of the pure Manc I left with, it was now infused with a strong and unmistakable Pakistani twang. I had learnt that my cousins and other kids in Sahiwal could understand me if I spoke English in an exaggerated, almost comical 'bud bud ding ding' Asian accent. So for the last month or so I had supplemented my broken Urdu and Punjabi hybrid with a borderline offensive Pakistani English. I just didn't realise that it would take a while to completely shake it off and go full Crumpsall again. At first my brother and sisters found it hilarious, ribbing me mercilessly when I said words like 'teleweeyan', 'wideo' and 'fillum' (which made going to Blockbusters a nightmare). But it became a bit more of a problem when I couldn't snap out of it by the time school started. This wasn't good. I was already very shy, and the last thing I needed when trying to fit into a new school – that was at least one social class above me and almost all white – was a Pakistani accent.

My trip to Pakistan had also left me weak and gaunt-looking. When I left Heathrow Airport in what felt like a lifetime ago, I was a round-faced kid with a toilet brush haircut and a healthy appetite for Opal Fruits and Smiths Crisps. But Pakistan changed all that. Playing football or cricket every day was a great form of exercise no doubt, but to do it so regularly when the Sahiwal sun was beating down on us wasn't the smartest idea. I had suffered from dehydration a couple of times as a result, once even requiring a saline drip to sort me out. I'd also succumbed to what can only be described as a monumental case of the shits on a few occasions, usually from eating street food that was extremely delicious but also painfully vengeful. So yes, my return to Manchester saw me half-fried, two shades darker, looking decidedly malnourished and sounding like Spike Milligan in a seventies sitcom. My brand new school uniform was already three sizes too big for me and now with my patented Pakistani weight loss plan I was practically drowning in cheap polyester.

Incidentally, it wasn't cheap. It was actually ridiculously expensive, a massive fucking con. Back then I think there was one or maybe two suppliers of the officially licensed Bury Grammar uniform and games kit and their absurd monopoly was reflected in a cost which was prohibitive for us, but of course my parents shelled out. I never even wanted to go to this posh-arsed school in the first place and yet here it was burning a hole in the family budget before it even started. I'd got in on a means tested 'assisted place', due to our low-income status, but that obviously didn't cover other expenses. At the same time Ayesha, who had previously gone to North Manchester High School in Moston (along with my other older sister Usmaa), was enrolling into the sixth form at Bury Grammar School for Girls, just across the road from the boys' school. She was far more into it than me, but I kind of got that. She'd excelled at North Manc-y and going to a grammar school sixth form was a natural stepping stone to going on to a decent university. I was miles away from that thinking; my immediate priority was getting myself some mates.

This is going to really age me but it was a time before Manchester had a tram system in place (the new one, not the one in the 1930s). So the route that is now a Metrolink service from Manchester to Bury was then a train. On my first day of high school, Ayesha and I were standing at Crumpsall station waiting for the train when we spotted an Asian woman looking at us from the other end of the platform. She was specifically squinting at my uniform. After a moment of recognition she made a beeline for us, with a kid my age in tow. He was wearing a puffy coat, but it turns out there was a Bury Grammar blazer underneath. She explained to my sister that it was her boy's first day at Bury Grammar too and asked whether he could sit with us so he wasn't travelling alone. Ayesha, being the unfailingly kind person she is, said of course and that we'd wait for him after school too. This new auntie (she was an 'auntie' now because she was Asian and we'd known her for 10 seconds) was very grateful and introduced her son as Sajid. Aware that I'd been resolutely mute the whole time, my sister introduced me as Ghazali (my parents had nicknamed me after the famous Islamic philosopher and theologian Al-Ghazali). I corrected her and said it was 'Nooruddean' (my birth name, meaning 'Light of the Faith'). Sajid looked too fed up to care and I instantly warmed to him. We'd quickly become best friends at school and proper mates outside of it too: the two common-as-muck Cheetham Hillbillies at Bury Grammar.

Upon arriving at Bury Grammar, Sajid and I were split up because of our names. I was in form room 1A and he was in 1Z, based on alphabetical order. I looked around and it was mostly all white, except for two or three of us brown lads. It was so different from primary school, which was so much more diverse. For instance there wasn't a single black kid. And no girls, which shouldn't have been a surprise for a boys' school but it still *looked* weird to me at first sight. Everyone seemed to know each other and I felt horribly out of place. I'm sure it was partly down to some of the new boys just being far more outgoing and confident than me and immediately striking up conversations with their new classmates, but a lot of them were friends already. Bury Grammar had its own infants and primary school and so naturally a good number of the high school intake fed through from there. I say 'infants', but they didn't call it that. Whereas Cravenwood had infants (which would be Year 3 in new money), and then Junior 1, Junior 2, Junior 3 and Junior 4 (by which time you were old enough to sit on the sports benches at the back of assembly rather than on the floor), Bury Grammar had, as far as I could tell, 'Introitus', 'Transitus I', 'Transitus II' and 'Exitus'. It all sounded like olden days Bible speak to me with a few Roman numerals thrown in. I asked a boy why they were called that and he said it was Latin. I said I didn't know Latin, and didn't know I needed to know Latin, and asked if he knew Latin. He said he knew enough and walked off to speak to someone less needy and weird.

I also clocked that there were different uniforms for different boys. It was basically the same but the school badge on the blazer pocket and the stripes on the tie came in different colours. Mine was green. I looked up and another Asian boy was also green. I started to wonder whether it was green for Pakistan but then noticed another Asian boy with light blue. I was mostly relieved but a bit disappointed. Turns out it was because we were in different 'houses'. There were four houses – Derby (yellow),

Howlett (red), Hulme (light blue) and Kay (green). I didn't know what houses were but immediately wanted to be in Howlett because of United, but found out we couldn't swap. At least I wasn't in Hulme. Kay was ... Celtic? Cameroon? It could be worse, I suppose. These days I would have had Harry Potter as a reference point but I related it back to PE at Cravenwood when we'd get split up into different coloured teams, which wasn't too removed from what it actually was I suppose. The school badge itself was not cool. It wasn't like the United badge with a red devil or Arsenal with a cannon. It looked like a duck or a swan choking on a key, which was a bit too close to a liver bird for my liking. Maybe not being in the red house was a lucky escape. Under the choking duck/swan/whatever was some more Latin – *Sanctas clavis fores aperit* – meaning 'The key opens sacred doors,' which sounded like something from *Indiana Jones*.

I found myself seated next to a lad called David Chaytow. He was everything I was not: smart, confident, handsome, suave (or as suave as an 11-year-old can be) and his dark wavy hair was immaculate, like Lee Sharpe or Paul Lake. Also his uniform fitted him perfectly, whereas I was drowning in mine (as it was to last me until I was old enough to vote). I checked David's house and he was yellow. I was suddenly desperate to be in Derby. The funny thing is, David and I were never really mates back then but he's one of the very few lads from school I've kept in touch with. He's been kind enough to reach out to me with words of support when I've really needed it and he's just a genuinely lovely and caring person. One thing I found especially weird about the boys who were catching up with each other from exodus (or whatever it was called) is how formally they referred to one another. They didn't use their first names. At primary school, as with every other part of my life so far, you called people you knew by their Christian (or Muslim) names. It was Nooruddean or Terence or Angela or Brendan. Or if we were *really* good friends, maybe even Ghazali. But here, they were all calling each other by their surnames. Little 11-year-olds saying stuff like 'What class is Goddard in?' and 'How was your holiday, Browning?' and 'Butterworth, who's that weird kid sitting next to Chaytow?' It was *so* odd. The type of stuff you'd hear in *Mary Poppins* or read in an old comic. Little did I know, while silently consumed with reverse snobbery, that I'd soon wish we'd stuck to second names.

The general chitter chatter of the classroom was in full flow when our new form teacher walked in. Immediately there was complete silence, but for the noise of 27 chairs scraping against the lacquered floor in unison. Everyone had automatically jumped to their feet as the teacher, Mr Robinson, marched across the front of the room and signalled for everyone to sit down. Of course I mimicked them, albeit ever so slightly late like a fan with bad knees in a Mexican wave. The whole thing reminded me of the time we went on a Cravenwood school trip to Wigan Pier and they had an old classroom mocked up with an actor playing a strict Victorian teacher (who was a bit too method and pulled Jamie up by his ear, to which Jamie responded with 'Owww! Fuuuck off!'). As much as the standing to attention business felt like something out of the *Beano* or the *Dandy*, it was a relief that Mr Robinson looked relatively normal. He wasn't wearing a black gown or mortarboard. It was just a normal suit and tie. The register was a weird situation where Mr Robinson only seemed to be in possession of our surnames and initials. So the roll call for attendance involved each of us confirming our presence and filling in the blank for our given name. I was nervous about this because I had a stutter, which got worse when I was nervous – and any sort of public speaking made me mega nervous. It turns out there was another boy called Alistair whose stutter was far worse than mine and when he valiantly stated his name after something of a struggle, no one laughed. So at least there was that.

As the names were read out one by one, with each boy stating their first name, I was surprised to hear that one of the other Asian boys was also called Choudry. Well, 'Chaudhari' to be exact, but still. What were the chances of that? Maybe we could be friends. Here come the Two Choudry's, they'd (possibly) say. He was asked to spell out his first name, Kaushal, because it was unusual, and he confidently obliged. Then it was my turn, and I too was asked to spell it out. With a deep breath so as not to stutter I blurted out 'N-Double-O-R-U-Double-D-E-A-N' as fast as possible. Mr Robinson was understandably whooshed and asked me to slow down and say it again. I heard a bit of laughter. Slower, and more deliberately, I said 'N-Double-O-R-U-Double-D-E-A-N'. This time I could hear a strong and unmistakable Pakistani accent as I spoke. Particularly when I said 'double' and 'R-U' with a hard R. This time the laughter had spread and was more obvious. Mr Robinson looked up with a wry smile and continued with the next boy. With my cheeks burning with embarrassment I looked up and saw Chaudhari with his chair turned to me laughing with the others. I was mortified and especially angry with him. I don't know why – what was he supposed to do? Still, I knew we wouldn't be mates. I cursed him and I cursed this stupid accent I'd picked up that wasn't even mine. I felt like telling everyone, 'No! No! I'm not from Pakistan! I'm from here! I'm from Manchester!' But what was the point? It would only come out in a Pakistani accent anyway.

The name spelling thing was repeated in each new class with each new teacher for the next couple of days. Every time, I dreaded my turn and there would be stifled laughter. It's not like the whole class was pointing and laughing at me, but even a slight guffaw each time felt like that. I realised repeating 'double' twice was a mistake. In breaks and between classes I'd have boys singing 'N double O double R double D' at me with a mock accent. I'm sure that to them it was harmless piss-taking but I was

reduced to one) so second place Aston Villa went into the European Cup and United, having won the FA Cup courtesy of a Lee Martin goal, went into the European Cup Winners' Cup. It was the first time I'd even fathomed us playing against European clubs. I'd read all about the Busby Babes and the Munich Disaster in 1958, and how Sir Matt Busby had rebuilt the team over the next decade to become the first English side to win the European Cup in 1968. I'd also seen pictures of George Best wearing a sombrero at the airport and Busby celebrating with the players at Wembley and even Bryan Robson being carried on the shoulders of fans after beating Barcelona in 1984. But I hadn't really considered why English clubs didn't play in Europe any more. I had to read up on what Heysel was and didn't realise English clubs had been banned from European competition until they were unbanned. But it was still incredibly exciting.

Even most of the teams making up the tournament were new to me. Of course I'd heard of European giants like Barcelona, Juventus and Aberdeen (because of Alex Ferguson) but the rest were a mystery box of discovery. They all had such cool-sounding names too. I mean, if you're used to a diet of Luton Town, Everton, Coventry City and Wimbledon, the possibility of facing the likes of Neuchâtel Xamax, Estrela da Amadora and Viking FK – a football club named after bloody vikings! – is like going from something as mundane as chips to something as exciting and exotic as peri-peri chips. In that respect, we absolutely lucked out in the first round draw with the best-named opponents in the whole competition – Pécsi Munkás of Hungary. All our games would be televised on ITV and that meant *The Match* with Elton Welsby, Brian Moore's gloriously growling commentary and Rod Argent's criminally underrated electric guitar intro music. I couldn't wait. These days we'd know everything there is to know about the Hungarian opposition, from the positional heat maps of their key players going into the game to a detailed dissection of their tactical setup. But back then there was none of that and xG was a type of Toyota. The best you'd get in terms of analysis would be a cheery Jimmy Greaves saying he didn't fancy their keeper much.

That might sound like I'm harking back to an ignorant Luddite past, but there's a lot to be said for the joy in discovering something new. I know it's not quite the same, but it's like avoiding any trailers or spoilers for a film you can't wait to see with fresh eyes. As a pure football fan – rather than a manager who's actually paid to know these things and implement strategies to deal with them – sometimes less is more. Even back then, proper aficionados could always grab a copy of the excellent *World Soccer* magazine that would profile foreign-based players and list all sorts of information about other leagues, but nothing could beat that anticipation of the unknown. For me, at the start of that first game in an exciting new European adventure for the team I loved, Pécsi Munkás could have been anything. For all I knew they could have been the finest team I'd ever lay eyes on. I mean, they weren't, they were a bit shit in the end but still. The first leg, and effectively the whole tie, was over as a competition in the first 17 minutes at Old Trafford as United took a two-goal lead. The perma-tanned Clayton Blackmore scored our first with an absolute rocket that swerved away from the keeper (who Jimmy Greaves would have been well within his rights not to fancy). He had a moustache and a mullet and was basically Paul Calf with dark hair. His every attempt at saving the ball was so half-arsed and cack-handed that I reckon I could have scored past him with my wrong foot. It was still massively exciting though – United were back in Europe.

Meanwhile, at school there were constant reminders that most of the boys around me were living completely different lives to me. Holidays were a big one. I was amazed at how well-travelled everyone was, and how many things they'd experienced. Don't get me wrong, I think it's so valuable to see the world and experience other cultures and hopefully become a more rounded and enriched person because of it. But I didn't expect kids my age to have been on safari or visited Mexico or having swum with dolphins. Someone mentioned the Northern lights and I thought, at last, something I can relate to; I'd been to Blackpool too. Skiing was a big thing for these mini Michael Palins. There was a lot of passing chat about it, and not even in a bragging, status way. It was just something that was taken for granted and clearly a regular pastime during half term because that's when talk of taking to the skiis would properly ramp up. I'd get asked where I was going and the honest answer would be downstairs from the flat to work in my dad's shop in Cheetham Precinct (I say 'work', it was more opening doors for people, fetching things from the back, bagging stuff up, and making tea for my dad's pals when they'd pop in).

That's why it was great having Sajid about because he'd be doing pretty much the same thing – helping his dad out on the markets. The one difference between Sajid and myself was that *his* dad would pay him a token amount for his efforts, whereas my dad's attitude to paying me was the same as his attitude to pocket money: putting food on the table and clothes on my back was 'payment' enough, thank you very much. There was even one time when he was watching *The Money Programme* on BBC Two and he quickly switched over when they started talking about average pocket money allowances, just in case I got uppity 'notions'.

Another identifier of the in-school class divide was dinner tickets. Because of our low-income status, I was eligible for what was essentially a strip of five blue raffle tickets that I'd collect at the start of each week and were worth a specific amount of money in the school canteen. It wasn't enough to cover the cost of a whole meal, but most of it. Maybe a pound or something. There was a bit of hesitancy on my dad's part to accept this natural extension of my assisted place. I didn't ask him about it directly but I suspect it felt instinctively too close to a 'hand-out'. In the end, there was an acceptance that needs must. Now, I could make a big thing about how mortified I was at having to use these repurposed raffle tickets to pay for my food; how it ate away at my working-class pride as I swallowed spoonfuls of unseasoned shame, each mouthful choking me with self-loathing. But it wasn't like that at all. I accepted them gladly and used them without a hint of embarrassment.

We've already established that I wasn't raking it in on the pocket money front and so the alternative to these dinner tickets was having to bring in a packed lunch of margarine sandwiches and ready salted crisps (which would obviously go straight into the sandwich). Having dinner tickets meant having school dinners, which was an absolute winner for me. I'm sure it's a sentiment shared by many a kid from an immigrant family, but you definitely go through a phase when you think of the delicious, beautifully flavoured, lovingly made food from home as somehow being inferior to the bland, beige, breadcrumbed foodstuffs your white mates are chowing on. So I saw this as one of the few pluses of being at Bury Grammar – chips, mash and a side of roast potatoes please. Obviously the other kids would clock that I was using dinner tickets to pay for my dinner but I wasn't really arsed about that. In any case, come Ramadan, they were still providing me with raffle tickets that I wasn't using, so I'd just sell them on to the rich kids and take their dinner money for free.

In any case, dinner (and we're using the established northern breakfast-dinner-tea definition here) was a fairly rushed affair, as we needed the maximum amount of time to do what the dinner break was really for – playing football. Well, a kind of football at least. Before I go on, I should warn you that this is going to sound incredibly made up. In fact it wouldn't be out of place in one of those *Monty Python* skits where they're sitting around and competing with each other about how poor they were growing up. But I promise you that there's no poetic licence taken. For a large chunk of our first year at Bury Grammar, Sajid and I would spend the majority of each dinnertime playing one-on-one football with a can. While other boys were using real balls and having a kick-about in the very same playground, we'd be essentially playing with rubbish. And voluntarily so. Each day we'd hurriedly scoff our subsidised carbs before heading out to the concrete plot of the playground we'd claimed to hunt down a discarded can of pop. We'd then stomp on it until it was a crumpled aluminium disc and we'd be away.

There was a cloak section of the school building with double doors that led out to the playground. These doors never opened but there was a step in front of them – that was our goal. So we'd both simultaneously be attacking and defending that step. If your mate took a shot and it deflected off you, it was your goal. We probably should have patented it as 'can ball' or 'foot can'. Goodness knows what the other boys thought as they witnessed us fighting for possession of our own kind of jagged Tango. The thing is, we obviously weren't so strapped for cash that we couldn't afford a real football – a cheap flyaway would have cost a couple of quid from the newsagent – but we just loved our shitty made-up game. And of course we gradually moved on to a more conventional playground kickabout. But honestly, when you were in full flow on a mazy run with a crushed can, haring towards that step/goal, you felt like Maradona.

By the time the Christmas holidays came around, United had successfully navigated their way to the quarter finals of the Cup Winners' Cup. After dispatching Pécsi Munkás without too much trouble, the next opponents on our exciting continental adventure were Wrexham. We beat them 5–0 on aggregate, including an uncharacteristic Gazza-esque dribble from Mark Hughes which won us a penalty – and even more freakishly, a perfectly executed thunderbastard from Gary Pallister from just inside the area. If Wrexham and Pécsi were relatively soft opposition to ease us back into Europe, next was our first major challenge. Fergie called Montpellier the 'real thing' and they'd already beaten Romario's PSV Eindhoven and walloped Steaua Bucharest twice. Unlike the previous rounds I'd actually heard of a couple of their players. Their captain was Laurent Blanc (many years before he joined us and a lifetime before he came out with grotesque comments about black players and female reporters as a manager) and a genuine superstar in Carlos Valderrama. I was buzzing about Valderrama because he'd featured in Italia '90 for Colombia and it felt like a big deal to have him come to Old Trafford. Except the state of our pitch was embarrassing, being all muddy and clumpy and horrible.

It was both a disappointment and a relief that Valderrama was injured for the first leg. United scored within seconds of the game starting thanks to a great run from Lee Sharpe and a sliding finish from Brian McClair, only for Lee Martin to level it with an own goal. They made a big deal about how away goals count double in the commentary and I had no clue what they were on about. The pitch was as bad as expected but the only real embarrassment was Hughes clutching his face after getting shoved in the chest by Pascal Baills, getting him sent off. So much for the 'foreign disease' and the 'dark arts' of continental players. The build-up to the second game was all about how angry Montpellier were about the red card and how hostile the reception at La Mosson would be. Valderrama was back too. It turned out to be a proper battle with loads of dirty fouls and over the ball challenges. They were after Hughes all game and he seemed to love it. Valderrama looked a class act every time he touched the ball but didn't really cause us too much bother. In the end another Clayton Blackmore special from like 200 miles out, which the keeper fumbled, and a penalty from Steve Bruce got us the win. It felt significant, like we'd achieved something of note against a proper side.

The semi-finals were us versus Legia Warsaw and Barcelona versus Juventus. We clearly had the kinder draw on paper and that's how it turned out. Unlike the previous ties, we were playing away first and a 3–1 win made the return tie a dead rubber. The one distinct memory I have of that first leg is a sign that was behind one of the goals. Bold as brass it had scrawled in big capital letters 'WHITE POWER' with a symbol of a circle with a cross in it. It flashed up a couple of times when the camera panned across with the action on the pitch. It freaked me out. I had to turn to my sister Usmaa to double-check that's what it said. She said it did, yeah. I wondered why it was allowed in the stadium and how it was okay for it to just be on telly during a game like that. Then an immediate fear hit me and I asked my sister if it was a United flag. She said don't be daft, it was *their* fans. It made beating their team that little bit sweeter. As for the other semi-final, I was desperate for Juve to win so we could play them in the final. The media were making a big deal about the fact that Mark Hughes used to play for Barcelona and so it would be the perfect final for him because he had a point to prove. With all due respect to Sparky I didn't really care about that. I just yearned for us to play against Toto Schillaci and Roberto Baggio. The former was *the* face of the World Cup along with Roger Milla and Gazza, and he brought all that glamour flooding back. The very sight of him rekindled memories of BBC montages set to 'Nessun Dorma'. The latter was Roberto fucking Baggio. He was so cool, so skilful and stylish. I think I was a bit in love with him. Alas Juve lost so it was Barça in the final. We were deprived of the Divine Ponytail.

What a final it was. I've watched the game so many times since, especially in the days and weeks immediately afterwards because I recorded it on VHS. We didn't have a spare tape handy so I just sellotaped the top of *Bedknobs and Broomsticks* and used that. The match wasn't exactly a classic in pure football terms but it was such an occasion. I remember seeing all the United flags where our fans were sitting behind the goal and feeling dead proud that we were in the final. Although I did wonder why we were playing in full white when they were wearing blue – maybe it was early Fergie mind games to fool them into thinking we were Real Madrid. We also had 'Sharp' missing off the front of our shirts like it was illegal in Rotterdam or something; it seemed strange at the time but it also turned that shirt into an instant classic. One of those anomaly kits you associate with a particularly special moment in history, like blue at Wembley in 1968.

Ahead of the game, a lot was made of Barça's superior technique and greater pedigree, and star names such as Michael Laudrup, Ronald Koeman, Jose Maria Bakero and Julio Salinas. And of course their manager, the legendary Johan Cruyff. In my mind's eye, he was that really cool-looking Dutch player from the old days I'd read so much about; a player so good they'd named a piece of skill after him. So I was a bit disappointed to see him looking rather dishevelled on the bench, wearing a massively oversized mac like he was Inspector Gadget's skinny little brother.

Just as with Montpellier, United played with zero fear. We gave Barcelona none of the respect that the media and pre-match build-up suggested we should. And it was dead right because they were no great shakes. We didn't play amazingly well but it always felt like we were the ones on the front foot and making things happen. They were always reacting to what we were doing and there was none of the silky one-touch passing we were told to expect. If anything it felt more like it was two English teams battling it out. Loads of bluster, each side needlessly giving away possession and nobody properly settling on the ball. We had a decent chance in the first half when Gary Pallister played a lovely through ball (eat your heart out, Koeman) to McClair but he skied it. But the game really came to life in the second half. Lee Sharpe was causing them all sorts of problems and you could tell Hughes was really up for it. But our first goal would have caused serious arguments on Cravenwood top pitch. Steve Bruce, who was scoring for fun that season, headed a Robson free-kick towards goal. It was going in too but Hughes toe-poked it right on the line. He stole Bruce's goal! Not that I really cared. I couldn't believe we were ahead.

Things got even better seven minutes later. Barcelona were playing a really high line and had nearly got caught out with another counter-attack when they lost the ball again. Robson dinked another lovely through-ball to Hughes who was clear. Their goalie Carles Busquets came sprinting out of his area sweeper-keeper style to slide tackle Hughes, who just about managed to toe it past him. But it meant he'd taken the ball miles out to the right wing and away from goal. With a couple of Barça defenders sprinting back to cover the vacated goal, it looked like the chance had gone, but then Hughes – the superhero that he was – powered the most perfect shot into the net from a stupid angle. The fans in the stadium (and me and my sister at home) went mad. The slow-motion replay remains one of the most beautiful things I've ever seen. The way Hughes, with utter conviction and without a hint of a doubt, absolutely leathers that ball with his body half-turned, and it curves perfectly into the net, a defender sliding in a millisecond too late – it's pure art.

Koeman scored from a free-kick with ten minutes to go, and Blackmore cleared off the line not long after, but I had no doubts that this was our time. As Robson lifted the trophy I cried with happiness. We were the Champions of Europe. Or the Champions of the Cup Winners of Europe or something. That wasn't important. It was a European trophy and we'd won it. More than the FA Cup, this felt like I was actually living one of those moments I'd only read about in books. This would be a page in future books about United and I'd just seen it happen. Fergie had a massive, goofy smile on his face as he mock conducted the fans in the ground. They sang 'Always Look on the Bright Side of Life' and Rotterdam was rocking.

5.

YOU WANNA LIVE LIKE COMMON PEOPLE

One thing I've always hated with a passion is working-class cosplay: the adoption of affectations and outfits by the middle classes (and above) to pass for a class lower than their own. It's a wilful and surface-level climb down the income ladder to a rung that they believe affords them a strange kind of credibility. It's the illusion of a tough life, or at least a life less cushy. As a kid it was more a visceral feeling of 'What are you acting like that for? That's not you?,' with a sense of bafflement as to why someone was suddenly behaving or dressing differently for no reason. With age and a better understanding of how common the act of faking common has become, I kind of get it to a certain extent. We all appropriate from other cultures and influences, whether we are always aware of it or not. It's part of human nature to mimic behaviours to fit into particular settings. But that innate survival instinct has a limit beyond which it's just gross, weird and offensive. Especially when, to quote a Mancunian icon turned embarrassing uncle, you just haven't earned it yet, baby.

There are certain traits and hangovers that anyone who has genuinely lived through any hardship recognises. The sickening reflex which momentarily greets a brown envelope falling through the letterbox; the involuntary little prayer that precedes a card going into the ATM because it has given you bad news so often in the past; that hollow feeling you experience every time you pass a pawn shop or Cash Converters and spot a toy or games console that had to be prised from small hands and sacrificed to pay an overdue bill. I still feel physically ill whenever I inadvertently flick over to a 'Can't Pay? We'll Take It Away' style show on the telly. Not to go into too much detail but I have twice experienced situations that involved either the heartless execution or imminent threat of bailiff action, once directly and once helping out a close friend's family. It's a uniquely desperate and numbing situation to go through; one that is void of any humanity and smothered in callous humiliation. If you've not had the misfortune to experience it, imagine someone breaking into your home and looking you dead in the eye as they take your things, safe in the knowledge that they have the law on their side. I wouldn't wish that on my worst enemy, and yet *Call the Bailiffs* and their ilk are broadcast as a form of disposable entertainment. They have no doubt been commissioned and produced by privileged types who have never had to face such dire straits and yet wear the pre-distressed T-shirts and chunky gold chains to suggest they did.

I'm only too aware that I had it far easier growing up than a lot of people I lived around and went to primary school with. I had two parents and a stable family for one, and my dad had an income (albeit less than steady) for most of my upbringing. There were times when I knocked on for mates or walked home with them after school and saw snapshots of just how dire their circumstances were. And I don't just mean in terms of poverty or desperate living conditions. There's a look a child gives you whenever home is mentioned or when they're just about to enter their front door which ages them years in an instant. It's a sudden dread and draining of all joy that tells you things just aren't right. Even as a kid you notice it. Back then you made a mental note not to mention it again so as not to upset them or ruin their mood, but hopefully these days there's more of an inclination to open up and ask what's wrong. As an adult I volunteered for a reading programme focused on disadvantaged areas in Manchester, to help primary school age children who were behind in their literacy levels. I was assigned to a school in Monsall and can honestly say that I got as much out of it as they did. But I could see a tiredness and premature weariness in the eyes of the kids I was working with that was at least partly due to malnutrition and/or unhealthy living conditions. It broke my heart to see them trying really hard to concentrate but struggling out of sheer exhaustion.

Growing up, we were never allowed to feel sorry for ourselves. Both my parents would be utterly mortified if we ever suggested we were less well off or poorer than anyone else. I think it's partly a working-class thing and partly an immigrant thing. The opposite of well-off people pretending to be poor is less well-off people disguising the fact. It's a shitty feeling to have less money, fewer opportunities and a dimmer future than other people, so why would you brag about it? It's not a badge of honour when you're living through it, nor does anyone praise you for your Balenciaga stylings if the soles of your shoes are coming off. It hurts your pride. There's a dignity to less well-off people not seeing poverty as dignified at all and rather holding tight to their self-respect. And if your family emigrated here from a former British colony, there's a whole added weight of insecurities and societal pressure to avoid at all costs the P-word ('poverty', not the other one). It was with a mix of ambition, bloody-mindedness and blatant delusion that I was brought up in a house where we were made to believe not having things was a choice rather than a circumstance – and also that the flat we rented above a fruit shop was our home.

My dad played a sort of Jedi mind trick on us growing up which fooled us into thinking everything we were denied was purely down to his discretion. He was always a dominating presence and strict in all sorts of ways, but looking back there was definitely an element of that which was born of our economic circumstances. He'd never admit to the fact that we couldn't afford a particular thing – it was always a waste of money compared to a cheaper alternative or a frivolity not worth bothering with at all. There were the more general things that we just resigned ourselves to as facts of life: no pocket money, no holidays beyond visiting relatives in Pakistan and definitely no takeaways. The one that surprises people the most whenever it crops up in conversation is a lack of birthday presents growing up. It elicits gasps of bewilderment and sympathy, but frankly it never bothered us. Well, it didn't bother me at least. Birthdays were never a big thing in our house. It was just another day. I think we assumed it was the same in most Asian households, or maybe it was just another Jedi mind trick. On the odd occasions any of us hankered for a specific thing, it required tact and low expectations. Be it a Thundercat figure or a Mr Frosty, Dad would usually rebuff the request, explaining why the thing you wanted was a waste of money by way of a two-hour lecture (if the lecture was a deterrent from asking in the first place it definitely worked). On occasion he'd do his best to attempt a money-saving workaround. In these instances he'd expect unbridled gratitude for his budget ingenuity, and if that wasn't forthcoming, it was time for another marathon lecture on the subject of ungrateful kids not knowing they're born.

To be honest we should have been grateful because at least he was trying to meet us half way. But we were just kids. And when you're a kid, little things are big in a way that adults don't understand. There's a fine line between cool and mortifyingly embarrassing. It's the difference between Nike trainers and Nicks knock-offs. To adults they're both just glorified pumps with a slightly different name. To their offspring it's the difference between being Michael Jordan and some loser who shops at Shoes Galore. Of course it did us no favours that we lived in Cheetham Hill, a.k.a. the counterfeit capital of the country (it's true, look it up). A whole generation of miffed young Mancunians walking around in Le Shark instead of Lacoste; Gallini in lieu of Benetton; and most depressingly, Winfield 4 stripes instead of Adidas 3. It also didn't help that my dad's great friend, Uncle Manzoor (I'd make a pithy comment about him not being our 'real' uncle but I love and respect him too much for that), owned a clothing wholesalers in town, so we'd often pop in to say hello after Friday prayers (where everyone removed far nicer trainers than me) and return home with Terry Wogan style jumpers and itchy slacks that were very well made but lacking in any street cred whatsoever. I wanted to *be* Michael J Fox, not interview him.

Even when it came to school, with its strict uniform code, my dad somehow found ways of unintentionally embarrassing me with his money-saving hacks. In future years, the Queer Eye gang would coin the phrase 'Clothes maketh the man but accessories maketh the man *fabulous*,' but back then, accessories maketh'd the young

Nooruddean cringeth. As with all the kids at the time, I yearned for a Head bag. Either the black holdall with red trim and gold detail (United colours obviously) or at the very least a rucksack with flourishes of fluorescent green or hot pink that I could wear on just one arm. The main thing was it had to be Head; or failing that, even a stand-ard sports brand like Nike, Adidas or Reebok would do. All of this made no sense to Dad, who had this mad idea that the singular purpose of a school bag was to carry things. So he popped into his shop and brushed off an old black JVC carrying bag. It basically looked like a flat suit-case made of floppy rubbery material. I was mortified yet had no choice but to lug it around like some sort of door-to-door salesman.

It was even worse when it came to footwear. I'd resigned myself to knock-off branded trainers for games and PE, but just wanted normal-looking black shoes to go with my everyday uniform. Kickers or Pods would have been the dream, but I could live without them. But my dad didn't see the point in buying a brand new pair of black leather shoes, when he could just pass down an old pair of his own – which were a size too big and *burgundy*. School shoes needed to be black with no exceptions and so my dad simply coloured them black with one of those spongy liquid polish things. He gave it a few coats and 'problem solved'. But pretty soon the polish started to peel off where they creased at the front (because they were too big) and it started to look like my black shoes were bleeding.

Another example of the disconnect between childhood longing and parental delivery concerned the local news-agents. I was at an age where I just wanted to soak up every last drop of football content out there. It was the days before the internet and prior to football properly exploding into the mainstream, so the 'content' in question was relatively scarce. There were a few appointment telly shows each week – *Saint and Greavsie*, a bit of *Grandstand*, *The Match*, the odd obscure foreign segment on TransWorld Sport – as well as actual hold-in-your-hand, ink-on-your-fingers written press. Looking back they were probably the glory days of football mags, before most of the titles were either digitised or rendered obsolete by online. You had your traditional staples such as *Match* and *Shoot*, the weekly pullout pink supplement of the *Manchester Evening News*, slightly more niche titles like *World Soccer*, and my favourite, *90 Minutes* magazine. *90 Minutes* was a bit more grown up and knowing than *Match* and *Shoot*, while still being fun and silly and not quite as cerebral and wordy as *When Saturday Comes*. Sort of like a precursor to *FourFourTwo*, except with fewer interviews and more gags. Each issue featured a really funny and topical comic strip by Nick Davies which I absolutely adored and turned to first, and their writers had their own personalities and in-jokes. I thought they must have the greatest job in the world in writing about football, having a laugh with each other and actually getting paid for it.

My dad didn't see the point. As far as he was concerned the newspaper had a sports section – there was football news and match reports in there. Surely that was all you needed to keep abreast of everything beyond the actual games? He just didn't see football as a viable hobby, never mind this all-consuming thing to obsess over. If I'd have expressed an interest in stamp collecting or birdwatching or something like that, I'm sure he'd have been far more amenable. But football? Nah. Still, he could see I was despondent and so arranged a workaround with the local Asian newsagents: at the end of each week we could come and collect a pile of unsold magazines that would otherwise be destined for the pulp. The slight snag for me was they never included a football mag. Ever. Instead it was the most random collection of publications you could hope to find. From puzzle books aimed at bored mums to part sixteen of a series on Victorian serial killers. One week it was *PC Zone* with the free CD missing, the next an out-of-date *Radio Times*. No *Match*, *Shoot*, *90 Minutes*, *World Soccer* – not even *Roy of the Rovers*. In fairness there was always the odd *Beano* or *Dandy* or *Whizzer and Chips*, which was a prize catch among the endless knitting patterns and obsolete TV listings. But overall it was not the ideal compromise.

Football was always seen as something of a frivolity. It wasn't like my dad was anti-football as such, he was just anti-football-costing-us-any-money. The exception being actual footballs. A favourite party trick of many an Asian dad at the time was to usher you over if you were ever in possession of a major brand football; with a knowing grin they'd ask you to check where the ball was made. It was nearly always Pakistan. As tenuous and random as this may seem, it was a genuine source of pride at a time when there were precious few visible exemplars of Pakistani contributions to popular culture. All these major stars around the world were playing with footballs sewn and stamped in the homeland. I remember my dad proudly boasting that prior to Maradona embarrassing Peter Shilton with the 'Hand of God', that very same football was first touched by the hand of a Pakistani. Granted, there was a slight disparity in how much each was getting paid for those touches, but I didn't have enough of a death wish to bring that up. The main thing was I was getting my own hands on a bona fide Adidas Tango – not an Adiddas Tongo or an Adadis Tanga but the real deal. While other lads were bringing their flyaways to the yard, I was rocking up with a legit casey and that meant you were in charge of the game. God bless my underpaid Pakistani brethren and sistren and their Singer sewing machines.

One thing that has always done my head in is when rich people look down on poor people for how they spend their money – be it brands, smart phones or even booze. Such sneering derision has always been around. In my day there was a peculiar obsession with the amount of satellite dishes on the sides of terraced housing, but if anything it's got worse with time. The gross residue of early 2000s 'chav-shaming' still coats perceptions of working-class life, while we live in an era of posh controversialists and right-wing politicians lecturing those forced to use food banks on how best to budget their lives. It can all be boiled down to one repugnant viewpoint: that people with scarce resources should not be allowed to experience joy, and should merely exist. Wake up, work, eat, shit and die. Or maybe just eat shit and die. There's even side-by-side memes of how a billionaire dresses versus how a 'chav' supposedly dresses; the former wearing a nondescript T-shirt and jeans and the latter dressed top-to-toe in expensive branded gear. Not only is it pathetically wide of the mark, but it suggests that the 'chav' (we never used the term in the north, it was always the far less disparaging 'scally') is wasting money on indulgences whereas the billionaire is not. It ignores the fact that rich people indulge in second homes, expensive cars, lavish lifestyles and nondescript T-shirts and jeans that cost thousands. If a less well-off person can't afford a quaint pile of bricks in the sticks, maybe it's okay for them to treat themselves to a nice new pair of trainers every once in a while. When you're poor, small status symbols like branded jackets or nice shoes or a fancy handbag are absolutely cherished, precisely because you've not got much else. Even on a superficial level, everyone needs that dopamine hit of treating themselves every once in a while, even if it's just on a pair of air pods.

It's hard to treat yourself when someone else is in charge of the money – especially when they get their kicks from sniffing out a cheaper alternative. But as ever, thank Allah for mums. While my dad was of the attitude 'Give a man a *Shoot* and he'll read it once, but give a man a *Gardener's Weekly* and he'll never ask you again', my mum bless her was altogether different gravy. She was just as nonplussed as my dad regarding my fixation with football and had even less spare money to play with. But she always did what little she could because she wanted to make me happy. It wasn't much considering our financial situation, but it meant the absolute world. From a very young age I'd accompany her to the local laundrette on Bury Old Road. We didn't have a washing machine so every week she and I would lug two or three black bags full of clothes with us to the Rainbow laundrette and spend a few hours filling up the loads for washing and then drying. I remember we'd spend the week between visits obsessively collecting enough 20 and 50 pence pieces to work the machines. Because so much of the routine involved sitting around and waiting for the cycles to finish – and on busy days just waiting for a spare machine – it could be a *looong* couple of hours. There was only so much jumping on only the black squares of the cracked chequered floor tiling I could do. And so my mum would give me some spare change (no precious 20s or 50s) and ask me to get her a *Bella* or *Woman's Own* – and a magazine and sweets for myself.

I was so buzzed. What had been a mind-numbing exercise in watching my sisters' shalwar kameez go round and round and round for hours on end became a lovely bit of me time with my favourite football weeklys. No pestering siblings or annoying distractions or Dad suggesting I do something more constructive with my time – just me, my mags and the occasional load/unload of washer drums. Every so often my mum would ask me how to spell a word for her puzzles and I was more than happy to oblige seeing as she had been so kind to me. If I was lucky, an old fella called Bob would pop in. I don't know how I knew his name was Bob because he never uttered a word or interacted with anyone. Come to think of it, maybe I made his name up. Anyway, he carried a portable radio around with him and would have local stations on with the football blaring out on full volume. I can't remember if it was GMR or Piccadilly Gold but I assume they didn't have the rights to broadcast full games because there was a lot of 'around the grounds' reports. Bless Bob for his disinterest in earphones or social etiquette because it was a dream for me to listen to football while reading about football. Rainbow went from a grubby laundrette to a multimedia football hub – like *Soccer Saturday* but with the warm, slightly musty smell of damp clothes and Daz Automatic.

An added bonus of football magazines was posters. Either A4 size or double page, they were one of the first things I'd leaf to just to see who they'd got. This is where the likes of *Match* and *Shoot* had the edge over *90* and their lives can go back to normal, and just at the end before the credits there's a shot of a tiny little baby monster scurrying past to set up the sequel? Well, that's silverfish. They lived down the side of my bed, in the cupboard room that housed the boiler, and at night, in the bathroom. It was fine during the day, but popping to the bog in the middle of the night was a mission. The cold tiled floor was like a Haçienda rave for the little bastards. My method was as follows: firstly, switch on the light to the bathroom and give it ten seconds, in the hope that the swarm of silverfish would be alerted to a giant person entering or would at least think it's daytime and piss off; secondly, enter the room emphatically and stomp about a bit without looking down, in the hope they scared themselves shitless by the now visible and earthquake-inducing presence of said giant person. Eventually, I'd be forced to look down and see the shimmering mob scrambling around aimlessly, some of them having the good manners to scarper to the edges of the skirting board or underneath the bath. Honestly, it knocked me sick and I never wanted to touch anything they'd touched.

As much as my mum was sympathetic to my wants at a time when money couldn't always stretch to all our needs, she couldn't justify my every whim. One thing I yearned for was a real Manchester United top – just like the ones the players wore. I'd longingly stare at the adverts in each week's magazines, usually modelled by Bryan Robson or Mark Hughes alongside a smiley young boy wearing matching clobber. I was so jealous of those little shits looking resplendent in branded polyester. Alas, football tops were just too expensive to countenance, and I fully appreciated that. But there was always the consolation of Lindy Lou down in the shopping precinct below us. Lindy Lou was a small independent shop run by an Indian couple, Ibrahim and Sara, who had emigrated over from Uganda in the 1960s. I say 'Ibrahim and Sara', it was actually 'Uncle Ibrahim' and 'Auntie Sara' because of course it was. They had no children of their own but were extra nice to us, always telling us how much we'd grown and how we'd be bigger than our mum before we knew it. I remember Auntie Sara even came up to the flat a few times to show my mum how to make mithai – gorgeous Asian sweets like barfi, ras malai, gulab jamun and laddu. All amazing colours and dripping with syrupy sweetness. It was diabetes denial of the tastiest kind, and probably a clever ploy to fatten us up so we'd need the next size up.

Lindy Lou specialised in unbranded childrenswear – the kind of thing you'd get in Woolies or George by ASDA. It was a favourite haunt of my mum's because their clothes were cheap, well-stocked and surprisingly hard-wearing. The latter was handy when shopping for me and my brother, seeing as we'd often end up with torn knees (both trouser and skin) as a result of over-exuberant kickabouts. Despite the fact it was such a small store – about the size of a small newsagents – they had a Tardis-like ability to find *something* akin to what you needed. Never quite perfect, but passable. The requested garment could always be found in some drawer or atop a shelf and Uncle Ibrahim and Auntie Sara instantly knew where. Jumpers, swimming costumes, massive winter coats, elasticated ties, ventriloquist's dummy style suits – you name it. Vitally for me, their infinite stock also happened to include football kits … of a fashion. They were incredibly unofficial and came in presentation boxes with see-through plastic windows like you'd get Asian clothes in. There was no attempt at a sponsor or manufacturers' logo but there was a club badge that you could sew on yourself. The badge itself was always embroidered quite nicely but it wasn't made of the puffy flock-style material you got on official replica shirts, which would fade and even start coming off after a few dozen washes.

Although they were very cheap and obvious knock-offs, with no 'Sharp' or 'Adidas' or interwoven 'MUFC' in the material, I still wore my fake-as-fuck Lindy Lou United strip with pride. This wasn't like wearing fake trainers or having to make do with 'Mr Scruffy' jeans instead of Mr Spliffy. There was none of that internal humiliation of not being quite on-brand. There was enough in that shiny red shirt, white trim and sewn-on, slightly malnourished devil to feel like you were wearing the real thing. The only feeling that any kid truly wants when wearing a replica football shirt is to feel as if they're part of the team. It is by definition not the real thing. You're not wearing it to impress your mates or to seem cool; it's not like your other clothes. It's more like cosplay than anything. In that shirt you *are* Lee Sharpe or Andrei Kanchelskis or [insert your childhood hero here]. You look *just* enough like the real thing to let your imagination do the rest. And granted, in a Lindy Lou top with no sponsor, no trefoil and a badge with visible thread between the lettering, I had to do a little extra imagining. But that was fine. I had a good imagination. Of course I'd have dearly loved an actual bona fide replica, but a barely passable snide was good enough. It's like when you're very young and you get a shiny new pair of trainers. You convince yourself you can somehow run faster and jump higher wearing them, and because you think it, you do. It's Dumbo holding his feather and flying.

The kit came with shorts and socks too, but even at that age I instinctively didn't want to be a full kit wanker and just wore the shirt. Plus the socks were made of the itchiest material known to man and were probably highly flammable. You'd end up with fourth-degree burns if you took them off too quickly. There was a Brucie bonus in the fact that the shorts came with an extra sew-on crest, so that could be used on another T-shirt or even your school bag. I never wore my fake United top for anything to do with school, but it was hardly off when it came to playing with my mates from round our way. Some of the lads had the Liverpool version, which I'm pretty sure was exactly the same top with a different badge supplied. No one was wearing City but maybe that's because even Lindy

Lou didn't stock them. Other kids wore United tops, the odd Pakistan cricket top and maybe even shalwar kameez depending on what day it was and whether they'd come straight from the mosque. You've no idea how difficult it is to try and nutmeg someone wearing a billowy shalwar akin to MC Hammer pants; your best course of action was just to outpace them, especially if they were wearing matching Bata sandals. All you could hear as you left them for dust was the forlorn slap of leather on heel. Sometimes we'd be joined by some white lads we knew from the area. They had shaved heads and were nearly always topless, even when it was cold. That seems a bit weird. Imagine telling an Asian mum you were leaving the house without a top on. You'd hear the sound of a leather sandal alright, but only as it smacked you on the back of the head with a shot accuracy Gary Lineker would be proud of.

As for going to actual games rather than playing in them, that wasn't really an option as far as my dad was concerned. Or my mum, to be fair. It was just accepted that I was too young to go unaccompanied by an adult, even though I knew lads at school who did just that with their pals. My parents didn't have the spare money or time to take me. Dad was busy with the shop and Mum was busy with everything else including all of us sprogs. And besides, a match day environment was so alien to my dad's world, never mind my mum's. Such a raucous 'white' atmosphere was a threatening prospect for them, and considering their experiences settling in this country, fair enough. Ticket prices were still relatively affordable compared to modern standards, but that was another barrier to entry for a world I was desperate to join. Eventually, I did end up going to the very odd game, but it was only ever with someone else's parents or a kindly friend of the family. It was painfully rare though and both my parents took a lot of convincing. They had to ensure I'd be safe and looked after in case some unpleasantness occurred. I was chaperoned to my first game by a lovely bloke called Fred. He wasn't especially into football but I think he took pity on the fact I'd never been. He was a tall, white, bald man with grey hair and I was a little brown boy. In other words a classic *Diff'rent Strokes* scenario. I'd love to say that every detail of that game is etched into my memory but it's not. I think it was Villa and I think we won 1–0. I was more engrossed with everything except what was happening on the pitch.

Old Trafford was two buses away but was like visiting a different country. Or a different reality inside the pages of a book. Arriving at the ground was strangely exotic considering the weather was just as shite and it was beside an industrial estate. Every smell, sight and sound was so in-your-face and intense. Fanzine sellers sporadically bellowing over the crowd; the deliciously greasy smell of onions and burgers frying from van to van; even the rumbling noise of such a mass of excited people crammed into one space was an assault on the senses. To my young eyes, the stadium felt massive, miles bigger than the Arndale Centre or the airport, even though it obviously wasn't. I was enthralled by the match day experience so much more than the actual game. Away from the ground, football was my obsession: the game itself, every player and all the nerdy details. But being there, on a match day, what happened on the pitch felt almost secondary. I was fervently people-watching in the knowledge that it could be months or even years before I was allowed to go again. Just random things like it was mad that all these adults were so openly swearing and it was no big deal. It wasn't intimidating or angry or anything, it was just done so casually. Funnily enough the one thing that did scare me a bit was the thunderous crack of noise and chaotic movement that greeted a goal. You no longer felt like a single person but instead part of a big wave. I bloody loved it. I felt like I belonged to something and yearned for the day when I could go to games on my own with my own money, instead of praying for those rare occasions when someone volunteered to take me.

6.

YOU'RE THE ONE FOR ME, ERIC

When I was still a nipper, I wrote to *Jim'll Fix It*. I was obsessed with any show that involved kids being able to do grown-up things. Watching *Why Don't You?* I was both in awe and rabid envy of the youngsters who got to present the show. *Press Gang* – with a very young Dexter Fletcher and Julia Sawalha – made me wish we had a school newspaper, while *Children's Ward* had me cursing the fact I wasn't in hospital with a terminal illness. The dance-happy kids on *Emu's All Live Pink Windmill Show* seemed a little bit much for me if I'm honest, but fair play for getting the gig. *Jim'll Fix It* was the ultimate, though.

The idea that you could write a letter to this Jim character and he could make your dreams come true was mind-blowing. Not only that, but every episode of the show was testament to the fact he could actually pull it off. Whether it was a little white girl getting to sing with

1980s reggae band Amazulu wearing a blonde dread-locked wig (yes, it was different times), or a group of cub scouts getting to eat sandwiches on a Blackpool roller-coaster, it was proof that Savile was capable of literally anything. After watching a kid get to be James Bond for the day, I was finally compelled to write in myself. Halfway through my letter, my sister Usmaa informed me it was dumb to ask for exactly the same thing and that they wouldn't let *me* be James Bond for the day too because they'd already done that. So I started again and asked Jim to fix it for me to experience zero gravity. Despite weeks upon weeks of giddy anticipation, I never got a reply.

In hindsight, that was probably for the best. As much as I believed that it was Savile himself who was pulling all the strings and making dreams come true rather than an army of production staff, the one thing that slightly put me off was meeting the man himself. Obviously I didn't know about everything that came to light in future years, but he did seem like a bit of a weirdo. Of course there were the peculiar affectations and strange outfits and dodgy white barnet, but there was something very unset-tling about the way he interacted with the kids on the show. They mostly seemed nervous and a bit uncertain and he was overbearing and vaguely creepy. I remember there was one young lad he picked out of the audience in a surprise reveal about a letter the boy had sent for some wish or other. While Savile was talking to him, he had a firm hold of his hair and was emphasising each syllable with a hard tug. The boy looked understandably freaked out. I didn't much fancy meeting Savile, but figured it was worth it to appear on the show and float around in a space rocket like Neil Armstrong or Charlie and Grandpa Joe in *Willy Wonka & the Chocolate Factory*. Besides, Savile was clearly a good guy. He was like Father Christmas except with actual video evidence of his gift-giving and magical abilities. Plus Savile was saving our lives with those horrific safety videos about kites getting stuck in electricity pylons. If anything, not wanting to meet him was more about my chronic shyness than anything else.

Of course, I should have trusted my gut instincts. Savile is perhaps one of the most extreme examples of icons who let you down badly. As much as his horrific behaviour was common knowledge and very much an open secret in showbiz circles, I honestly don't think that permeated down to the general public. We can look at the knowing references on the likes of *Have I Got News for You*, *Fantasy Football League* and the very 1990s *This Morning With Richard Not Judy*, and we can fool ourselves into thinking we all kind of knew deep down. But I don't think we did in Savile's case. It was an industry in-joke that we only got years later. There may have been an accepted consensus that he was an oddball of sorts, but not the monstrous fiend we now know him to be. If anything he was seen as more eccentric than evil, but we've transposed the new context onto our memories. That's the thing with don't like or a rival manager is reason enough to go off them. So for instance, Brian Kidd with a mop of black (or mostly black) hair is a Manchester United legend and European Cup winner who went on to become Sir Alex Ferguson's longest-serving assistant manager during a glorious period in the club's history. But there's another, slightly more portly Brian Kidd, who looks sort of similar but with grey to white hair who was part of Manchester City's coaching staff between 2009 and 2021. That guy can do one.

There's a plethora of other examples. There is one Michel Platini who graced both Juventus and France with insouciant elegance and movie star curls, making the untucked shirt and half-mast socks the unofficial uniform of the mercurial playmaker. There is an altogether separate Michel Platini who skulked the corridors of power at UEFA with bad intentions and an ill-fitting suit who was eventually found guilty of ethics violations and barred from sport until 2023. They clearly aren't the same guy. It's pure coincidence or some glitch in the matrix. Similarly, it's just deeply unfortunate that the outrageous 1990s talent that is Matt Le Tissier – a player so gifted and fantastical that he could casually pluck the moon from the sky and volley it into the top corner if he could be arsed – has a modern-day namesake who regularly questions the legitimacy of the war for Ukraine and scoffs at the notion of a global pandemic. In fact, the only cover-up truly worth contemplating is how someone managed to steal the Southampton legend's identity without anyone noticing. It adds credence to the kind of conspiracy theories that are baked into the more obsessive edges of music fandom, for example; that Paul McCartney died on 9 November 1966 and was secretly replaced by a lookalike with the remarkable ability to sing and write songs just as well. Or that the original Avril Lavigne was replaced by a body and voice double called Melissa Vandella. The clues are always there, in the songs and the album covers and awful *Soccer Saturday* takes.

Le Tissier's fall from grace and all conventional rationality is sad, of course, but from a personal point of view he was always someone I admired rather than loved. That said, I definitely included him in a few scribbled down Manchester United XIs I'd devise in the back of exercise books, assuming I'd been given charge of the club's summer transfer spending and knew far better than Fergie how to strengthen the team. He was a favourite addition to my squad, along with the likes of Earl Barrett from Oldham, Gabriel Batistuta from Fiorentina, Jay-Jay Okocha from Bolton, and Paolo Di Canio from West Ham. The last one very nearly happened in real life but was probably a bullet dodged in hindsight, what with the whole fascist sympathising thing (tattoos, salutes and all). A harder one to come to terms with was hero turned bitter Ailsa Stewart lookalike Mark Hughes. Sparky defined my early years as a United devotee. His thunder thighs, spectacular volleys, gravity-defying scissor-kicks and indomitable arse punctuated some of my most treasured memories as a mad little red. But then, he left us and stopped giving a shiny shit. One of the first daggers was when he started raving about Chelsea when he joined them, saying they were his childhood club and how it was a dream come true. Then came a drip-drip-drip of resentment and bitterness he felt towards United in general. The final betrayal was of course going on to manage City. In an act of collective cognitive dissonance, we started to call this new charlatan by his middle name of 'Leslie' instead of Mark to somehow preserve the memories of our beloved Sparky.

Top 5 Players I Wish United Had Signed

5) Jay-Jay Okocha: I think football fans these days are way too consumed with the end result. They want to win by any means necessary, and so much of that is fuelled by social media. It's not even about how winning makes them feel, it's about out-bantering a stranger on Twitter and claiming that a faceless adversary and their team of choice are 'in the mud'. Football should always be about how it makes you feel inside rather than what stats you can reference to top trump someone else. Jay-Jay Okocha was pure footballing joy to me. He could do things with a ball that took three replays and a lie down to properly understand.

4) Rui Costa: The Suede to Luis Figo's Oasis. His more revered compatriot may have had more money and accolades (and pigs' heads) thrown at him, but Rui was always the cool one. With his socks at half-mast and his shirt lazily hanging out at the hip, he always looked like a rockstar who'd decided to join the local kickabout. The way he moved around the pitch was so effortless and stylish, and then he'd get the ball and produce a slide-rule pass or a darting run that would change the game. He cared far more about creating goals for others than scoring them himself, because when you're *that* cool, who needs the extra attention?

3) Duncan Ferguson: I've always been slightly obsessed with Big Dunc. Some may find his inclusion in this list a bit incongruous, but I loved everything about him. There's a reason why fans have adored him wherever he's played. Of course he was a menace in the air and physical handful for any defender, but he could fucking play too. Old Trafford would have buzzed off him. How can you not love a man who keeps pigeons, does loads of great work for children's charities and *twice* hospitalised dafties who were stupid/brave enough to try and burgle his home? Tremendous.

2) Roberto Baggio: Baggio achieved so much in his glittering career and played for so many massive clubs, and yet there is still a lingering sense of what could have been. There are various sliding doors moments that didn't quite work out in his favour, from serious injuries to unappreciative coaches to missed penalties, but of course all that just makes his story more romantic. I think I was a bit in love with him, and would get a warm glow inside if United were even mentioned in the same breath (or flashing TeamTalk headline) as him.

1) Gabriel Batistuta: The greatest purveyor of the thunderbastard in all of Christendom, Batistuta scored the type of goals we all dreamt of in our sleep. The fact that he didn't take penalties felt like a health and safety regulation brought in by the goalkeepers' union. I was just in awe of him. In fairness I was in awe of anything to do with Italian football, thanks to Channel 4 and James Richardson, but Batigol was by far the biggest special effect in the GCU (*Golazzo* cinematic universe).

Going to City as an act of betrayal is a curious one. A surprising number of United players and staff of that era crossed the proverbial aisle, but with vastly differing impacts on their legacies. Although it was a big deal back then, it didn't have quite the same impact as it would have in future years. The context and relative fortunes of each club were just a little bit different. With all due respect to that version of City, they were a rival only in a parochial, tribal sense. They certainly weren't a direct sporting rival. So I suppose to a player, it was practical consideration to swap red for blue. They were already settled in the area, probably had kids in local schools, and City were a big club with a relatively good wage for the last few years of your career. You just had to keep your head down, not do or say anything antagonistic or stupid, and you could just about get away with it. Which brings us to Peter Bolesław Schmeichel. A player who was as integral to our 1990s glory years as anyone. There are all sorts of conflicting ideas about what the term 'world-class' means – the only real consensus is that it is used far too liberally. But of all the players United boasted in that first decade of Ferguson-era dominance, Schmeichel had the strongest and most undisputed claim to that title. He shared the dressing room with great players, and possibly greater players than him in a United context, but at his sustained best he was the finest goalkeeper in the world and one of the greatest ever. As such, he should be revered and loved as a United fans' favourite. Except, well, he fucked it by what he did in a City shirt.

I felt let down when he joined City in the first place. Obviously because he was going to *them*, but also because it was so unexpected and felt like he'd timed his departure from us perfectly. There's leaving on a high and there's leaving straight after winning an unprecedented treble and captaining your club to its first European Cup in 31 years. To call it a day after the most successful season in the history of a club the size of Manchester United is a flex and a half. It was gutting to hear the news but, fair play, he went with our best wishes. It sounded like he was off to semi-retirement in sunny Portugal too. That's no disrespect to Sporting Clube de Portugal (or Sporting Lisbon as we used to call it), but that's how it was sold to us in the press. Like a big shire horse had been retired after years of dutiful service and would spend the rest of its days happily grazing on lush fields with the sun on its unfettered back. But after winning the league at Sporting (their first for 18 years) in his first season, he decided to sack off his happily ever after and come back to England. It felt a bit strange that he'd be playing for another Premier League side; even the thought of him in an Aston Villa shirt felt wrong. But whatever, we had to move on with our brand new World Cup and European Championship winning goalie Fabien Barthez. Sure, we'd had a false start with Mark Bosnich, but with Barthez surely we'd sorted the problem of how to replace Big Pete once and for all. Plus he was going out with Linda Evangelista, so there was always the added bonus of potentially bumping into her on Market Street.

Schmeichel played against us three times that season – twice in the league and once in the FA Cup third round. An indicator of just how difficult properly replacing him would prove to be is that those games were split between that's football. Loads of players have careers that continue on after United. I was still full of good vibes for him. So much so that I was chuffed for him when he scored a goal for Villa against Everton at Goodison Park. It was a consolation, but what a strike. Van Nistelrooy would have been proud of the way he readjusted his feet and boshed it home. It brought to mind the header he scored for us against Rotor Volgograd in 1995 in the UEFA Cup (another consolation because it didn't stop us going out), and a stunning mid-air goal he scored with the outside of his foot against Wimbledon in 1997 that was a matter of inches offside. And of course there was the crucial bit of uncertainty he caused when he ran the length of the pitch for a certain Beckham corner in 1999. Anyway I'm getting ahead of myself. The point is, the streets don't forget. And I certainly hadn't forgotten the memories that Schmeiks had given us over the years. I always had a huge personal soft spot for the slightly unhinged no-shits-given cocks-out cockney chutzpah that Les Sealey brought to the position, but after Big Les, Schmeichel was the one. I loved the oft-repeated fact about him that it was actually a stint playing handball rather than football that honed his ability to psych out and smother one-on-ones with opposition attackers, thanks to his trademark star jump technique. Imagine a 6 ft 3 in, 16-stone Dane spread out like a demented sugar glider standing between you and the back of the net. You'd be forgiven for skewing it wide and ducking for cover.

Alas, hopes and dreams are there to be shat on. To paraphrase a certain celebrity City fan: 'Please don't put your life in the hands of a giant blond man, who'll throw it all away.' Because that's precisely where Schmeichel decided to rock up next. City had just been promoted back up to the Premier League and Kevin Keegan went on a wild £40 million spending blitz (admittedly United spent all of that amount on just one major signing that summer – Rio Ferdinand). City's most high-profile arrival was Nicolas Anelka from Paris Saint-Germain for £13 million, after a successful loan period at Liverpool. It was before PSG were PSG and City were City so there wasn't a drop of oil or petrodollar in sight. Happy days. There was also Robbie Fowler from Leeds, Matías Vuoso from Independiente (who cost around £7 million and never played for them), Sylvain Distin from PSG, David Sommeil from Bordeaux, Marc-Vivien Foe on loan from Lyon (their French scouts must have been working overtime) and a certain P Schmeichel from Aston Villa. What the fuck! One minute he's retiring, then he's semi-retiring, then he's back in the Premier League and then he's at chuffing City?! It was like he'd plucked out my still beating heart with one of those giant Reusch gloves, bounced it twice and absolutely leathered it into oblivion. Why couldn't he just have stayed with us for an extra two years, instead of us faffing about with Bosnich, Barthez, Carroll and the admittedly very handsome Raimond van der Gouw?

The first derby of the season was the last ever at Maine Road so there was all sorts of hype and sentimentality around it. Truth be told it felt like the end of an era for United fans too, but it wasn't a day for hands-across-town love and harmony. They were massively up for it and we'd started the season like it was us who'd just got promoted. It was only the second week of November and we'd already dropped points in six of our 12 games. The sight of Schmeichel in a City shirt was frankly grotesque. Before the game there was the famous moment when Schmeichel tapped Gary Neville on the shoulder in the tunnel and Neville, upon seeing who it was, refused to acknowledge him. Sadly it was our skipper's best moment of the day. Anelka scored within the first five minutes, courtesy of a weak Barthez parry from a Shaun Goater shot. Thankfully United equalised soon after as Solskjaer poked a Giggs cross past Schmeichel (which still sounds weird). Then Neville had a brainfart moment trying to shepherd a nothing ball out of play and Goater robbed him to put them in the lead again. Goater got his second and City's third in the second half after Ferdinand messed up this time by giving the ball away. We were a hot mess at the back without you-know-who. Maybe I was project-ing (in fact I definitely was) but every time Schmeichel made a save he seemed to have an almost apologetic look on his face like, sorry lads I have to do this. But all that was dashed at full-time when he besmirched his United legacy forever by doing a cartwheel in celebration. You motions in a professional manner and there was a kind of silent pact that we'd never speak of it again. That's why if I ask you now to imagine Cole in a City shirt, you can't.

Of course, a football 'cancellation' is a million miles away from real-life cancellation, in much the same way that football 'hatred' is (mostly) a very different thing to real hatred. When the great Bill Shankly uttered the immortal line: 'Some people believe football is a matter of life and death, I am very disappointed with that attitude. I can assure you it is much, much more important than that,' little did he know it would be so often misquoted and terribly misunderstood. Anyone who thinks Shankly was actually being literal knows very little about the man's wry humour and excellent politics. Being let down by a player for a footballing 'betrayal' isn't even in the same universe as a hero destroying your picture of them by being a horrible person. For example, what Schmeichel did in a City shirt pales in comparison to how bitterly let down I felt when Paul Ince went to Liverpool. Not only did Ince absolutely and positively buy into his new Scouse identity – fuelled by a seething animosity towards Fergie and his famous 'Big time Charlie' tag – but his celebrations after scoring against us at Anfield were so vitriolic and pointed they could have burned down the Golden Gate Bridge. However, that doesn't really make me think any less of Ince as a person. I appreciate he's a professional footballer with no inherent allegiance to the club I love, understand how he may have felt spurned by

Ferguson and United, and can see things from his point of view. It's infinitely harder to take when someone you've put on a pedestal offends your key pillars.

Two cultural icons I revered perhaps more than any others growing up were Eric Cantona and Steven Patrick Morrissey. Being from Manchester, it was perhaps inevitable that I'd pluck my heroes from the worlds of football and music. Maybe if I was from Twickenham, it would have been Vince Cable and Will Carling. Or the inventor of red trousers. But no, it was two walking egos with dark quiffs and a penchant for courting controversy. On the surface they had a lot in common and I could legitimately be accused of having a type. They were both of immigrant stock – Cantona's mother and paternal grandfather emigrating to France from Catalonia and Sardinia respectively, with Morrissey's parents heralding from Ireland; for good or for bad, each came to be defined by their relationship with the city of Manchester, regardless of where fame and fortune took them; and both were self-styled enigmas with a wit and idiosyncratic way with words that made them endlessly quotable. They were also proud contrarians who took great delight in putting noses out of joint and making a mess of convention. And, of course, they each had exceptional gifts in their chosen vocations that singled them out from the dreary sameness of normality. All that appealed to me enormously as someone who always felt different – because I often *was* different – but didn't want it to be a bad thing. I yearned to be as cool as either of them and as brave as both of them in being who I wanted to be – even though I was never a footballer and couldn't hold a note to save my life.

I do wonder whether the whole intoxicating aura around Cantona somewhat overshadows how good he was. It all starts to feel a bit ethereal and gaseous in terms of his actual contribution to Manchester United's 1990s rebirth. Like overblown fan fiction or a Che Guevara T-shirt, so overproduced and ubiquitous that it loses all meaning. As well as being an artist and a poet and all those other things, Cantona was everything you'd want in a striker. He was tall, strong, hard as fuck, technically superb and hardly ever made a mistake with the ball. That last one is such an important quality. It's about having the footballing IQ to know exactly what to do in any given situation, and the necessary calmness, spacial awareness and touch to pull it off. Dwight Yorke was another player who just never wasted a ball. Another thing about Eric that people don't always appreciate was his speed. Although hardly in the same bracket as a Lee Sharpe or Andrei Kanchelskis or David Bellion, he was deceptively fast. It was always apparent when he'd race into the opposition half on a counterattack or carry the ball through the high line of defence: rarely was he ever caught by a defender desperate to make up the yards. He was much bigger in the flesh too. It wasn't until you saw him at a game that you realised what a unit he was. Even taking away all the creativity – the little flicks and gorgeous dinks and sumptuous wedged finishes – he was a wonderfully complete centre-forward. The number of vital equalisers and winning goals that man scored in the tightest of games. He was always the difference, always providing those really tangible and evidential key contributions as well as all that fantasy.

Of course it was the fantasy that made you truly love him. One of the most beautiful sounds at a game of football is hearing an entire stand of people, and sometimes a whole stadium, let out an audible gasp of disbelief at what they have just seen. It doesn't need to be a big moment like a stunning goal or perfect through ball. It can be as small as a feint or a dummy or a piece of control. The thing is, we as fans in the stands or watching on telly can see things that the players can't. We get the bigger picture and spot runs or spaces opening up that it would be impossible for a player at ground level to always discover in time. But the gasp comes from something unexpected that we hadn't even imagined was a possibility. Cantona induced more loud sighs on a regular basis than an Asian son telling his parents he didn't want to study medicine or law. And that's not even taking into account everything he was off the pitch. He was referencing Molière, quoting the works of Arthur Rimbaud and listing 'art' as his favourite hobby outside football in an era when Graeme Le Saux faced homophobic slurs simply for reading the *Guardian* newspaper. It wasn't merely that Cantona didn't give a shit what people thought; I think he got off on being different and the English football media trying to work him out. There is no doubt in my mind that he played up to his persona on occasions and said certain things with the sole purpose of fucking with the collective minds of broadsheet journalists desperate to find deep meaning where there was none. I always found that overlooked aspect of Cantona – his humour – massively appealing. He took himself seriously but not half as seriously as others did.

Top 5 favourite United players from the 1990s

5) Les Sealey: Les had two short stints at United, and only one season as a regular first-team starter. And yet that was enough to cement him as a cult hero. He was an absolute barmpot in the best possible way; anything he lacked in stature or even technical ability he more than made up for in chutzpah and determination. My enduring memory of him will always be his angry refusal to leave the pitch in the 1991 League Cup final, despite the fact he was only propped up by one-and-a-half working legs. Big Les sadly died at the age I am now. RIP.

4) Denis Irwin: It's hardly a spoiler but Irwin is one of two Corkonians on my list. As much as I admire and massively rate the likes of Patrice Evra and Alexander Büttner, neither holds a candle to our Denis. He's often described as Mr Dependable and a solid 8/10 player, but that does him a gross disservice. In the modern era of solid full-backs and offensive wing-backs, he was a man who could do both. It was a joy to see him marauding down the left flank, to either send over a dangerous cross or come inside and hit one like a rocket.

3) Andrei Kanchelskis: I think I've already made it very clear that Andrei and I share a special bond (that he may or may not be aware of), but for me he was and is the archetypal Manchester United winger. He could see a cute pass, he could finish with aplomb and he was always capable of swinging over a deadly cross, but more than all of that he could dribble. To beat your man with a sleight-of-foot magic trick is the most thrilling and cruelly emasculating act in football, and Andrei was the Paul Daniels of wide players.

2) Roy Keane: It is often said that Roy Keane is one of the most underrated highly-rated players out there, in that his intimidating aura and combative edge tends to overshadow what a fine footballer he was. And that's true: Keane's technical abilities as an all-round midfielder were second to none, and his tactical nous helped him to evolve from a box-to-box tyro to the deep-lying metronome in later years. But I love him because he was as hard as fuck and scared people. And if you disagree, I'll see you out there.

1) Eric Cantona: Of course it could only ever be Cantona. The coolest, most magnificent bastard to ever set foot on the hallowed turf. The thing with Eric is that he was everything to everyone. Some people love a dangerous hardman; others prefer a delicate artist. There are those who appreciate clinical finishers, and then ardent devotees of free expression. Cantona managed to satisfy each and every erogenous zone, and some you didn't even know existed. I know Liverpool fans who hate everything and everyone related to Manchester United – but for one man. Please, please, please, don't ever let me down, Eric.

It's something I loved about Morrissey too. Granted Morrissey really did take himself very seriously, but there was often a tongue-in-cheek quality to his stuff that was often missed. What many bemoaned as depressing or morose in his songs, I found hilariously overblown and melodramatic. His lyrics made me laugh rather than bringing me down; like the stereotypical Smiths fan, I felt that they spoke to me more deeply than anyone else. And loved the fact that they were so different from any other type of music I was accustomed to.

Really, I was too young for the Smiths. I was but an infant during their heyday and only eight when they split. But a combination of my sister Usmaa being a fan and Abraham Moss library having a music section meant I was able to discover them after the fact. Apologies to Alan Partridge, but if you were to ask me then what my favourite album was, I'd have had to say 'The Best of the Smiths Vol. 1' and 'The Best of the Smiths Vol. 2' (I think they were actually called 'Best I' and 'Best II') because those were the cassettes Abraham Moss had in stock. The covers were two halves of Dennis Hopper's 'Biker Couple'. They also had 'The Queen Is Dead' but that only had ten songs on it compared to twenty-eight on the two 'Best Ofs' – and crucially they could be taken out together as one borrow on your library card. So weirdly, for me, the definitive Smiths track listing is one devised by some suit at Warner Bros for a money-making reissue, rather than one lovingly crafted by Morrissey/Marr.

My love of the Smiths was very different to my love of United. It wasn't communal and it wasn't about being part of some movement. The Smiths were personal for me; I got to know them in my own bubble. I had no hankering to meet fellow Smiths fans, mainly because they'd have been a decade older than me and that would have been a bit noncey on their part. But also, I've never looked at a group of Smiths fans and immediately thought: 'They're my people.' There's even a Smiths music video, for 'Stop Me If You Think You've Heard This One Before', which features Morrissey cycling around Manchester and Salford with a group of fans riding around like his disciples. Each of them looks like more of a wet wipe than the last; all are dressed in NHS specs and matching cardigans with their daft little Moz-a-like quiffs. Every so often there's a close-up of one of them looking forlornly at a photo of Oscar Wilde. It's honestly like a recruitment video for school bullies.

As much as I loved Morrissey and the fact he looks so different with his tall hair, billowy blouse, hearing aid and gladioli poking out of his back pocket, that was for him not me. And I certainly didn't want to be part of his twee little Moz Army. In fact the only thing I related to in that video was a shot of a traffic sign that said Cheetham Hill was a quarter of a mile away. In later years I saw Morrissey live a few times, most notably at his big comeback gig at the MEN Arena. It was great. I loved the music, buzzed off the performance, but then I'd look at people around me and think 'Nah, we like the same thing but I'm not one of you.' I went to Smiths nights at the Star and Garter a few times too and that was alright, but again, not really my scene.

That takes nothing away from how much I loved the Smiths and Morrissey in particular. Stripping back all the affectations and stylistic flourishes, his lyrics could be so beautiful. When you're bang in the middle of your difficult adolescent years, the appeal of someone making loneliness and isolation sound poetic and even cinematic is immense. You're in a constant state of thinking you're the main character of a film you're in, and for me Morrissey provided the perfect soundtrack. Away from the music, I loved how acerbic and cutting he could be in interviews, and how everything popular and mainstream was deathly dull and just the absolute worst for him. It was also extremely appealing to hear him voice his contempt for authority at any given opportunity and purposely rub people up the wrong way. Inevitably, as a fan, you get into a pattern of defending what he's saying and justifying his every shocking proclamation. He didn't mean it like that; it was tongue-in-cheek; he's actually making the opposite point but in a really subversive way. And that's fine up to a point.

Some Morrissey fans have always defended his every utterance and always will. That's their prerogative. But plenty have gone through the same trauma of difficult realisation I have: that Morrissey is in fact a bit of a tit. It's like that bit at the end of *The Usual Suspects* when he's looking at his noticeboard and suddenly all the various clues start to make sense. Eventually, the Kobayashi mug has to drop.

I loved Morrissey and I loved Cantona, and in my head there was an overlap of icons. But in the most fundamental of ways, they could not be more different. The footballer's heart is open and full of love; I find the singer's closed and filled with hate towards those who don't share his views. And in every instance, Cantona always says the right thing. Following the Charlie Hebdo shooting in 2015, he urged the public not to use the tragedy as an excuse to attack Muslims or their faith. 'What I want to say is that today, what just happened doesn't have to be used against Islam,' he told EuroNews. 'The danger would be to say that all Muslims are like that. It's important not to say that a Muslim is "moderate", if he's just a citizen like you or me. What does "moderate" mean anyway? Does it mean that Islam is an extremist religion? This is a latent provocation.' Our Eric has an inclusive and tolerant world view, saying 'I don't believe in regions. I don't believe in countries or borders. Because people start with a country, and then zoom into a region, then a city, then a street, then their family, and then themselves. I prefer to zoom out.' That's the difference between a hero who remains a hero, and one who crosses a line: I've never had to make excuses for Cantona. Even when – *especially* when – he kicked the hooligan at Palace for spouting xenophobic bile.

It's funny how your perception of the same thing can change over time. I remember watching footage of an old TV show called *Eight Days a Week*, which invited a panel of three celebrities to review music, movies and books. They had Morrissey appearing alongside George Michael and Tony Blackburn. They reviewed Everything But the Girl, a movie called *Breakdance*, a book about New Order and a recently discovered old recording by doo-wop group

7.

ALWAYS THE CARLTON, NEVER THE WILL

There's a certain second-generation accent that definitely doesn't sound foreign but at the same time doesn't belong to a white person. It has very little in common with someone born in Pakistan or India or anywhere in the subcontinent, but it is unmistakably coming out of the mouth of a British Asian.

There are a few elements passed down from the previous generation, such as for example the unintentional transposing of 'v' and 'w' to say 'wideo' and 'wery' instead of video and very, 'vy' and 'vimbledon' instead of why and Wimbledon. But it's not as deliberate – and far less mindful about pronouncing every single consonant – as the type of English accent that 'desi' immigrants (i.e. those from the Indian subcontinent) adopted to make themselves properly understood in their second and often third language. It's faster, more cocksure and chips off most of the H's and T's. It's always garnished with a number of 'innit's and 'yagetme's and even the old school 'Raaaaaaas!' Without wanting to generalise it's the sort of accent you might hear if you want to get your phone unblocked from its current provider, or if you were to ring up a call centre (in Bury, not Bangalore) to upgrade your current model at the end of its contract. Although they'd likely thank you for calling 'Carphone Varehouse' and suggest you switch your tariff to the new 'Wodafone' plan. If you've seen the excellent TV series *Man Like Mobeen*, a version of it is spoken by Tez Ilyas as the character called Eight. I've heard it referred to as an Asian 'rudeboy' accent (which is in itself appropriated from Jamaican culture) but it's not really. It's not just the preserve of mouthy lads who drive up and down the Curry Mile making a racket on Eid. It is – or was – much more common than that.

I don't speak in that accent and never really have. If you were to talk to me on the phone, I'm not sure you'd even recognise I was Asian more than clocking I was from Northern England and from Manchester. But a lot of my mates growing up in Cheetham Hill had a version of that accent. And it was obvious when we were talking to each other that my accent was different. I'd love to paint some sort of between-two-worlds Eliza Doolittle tale of how going to a grammar school robbed me of my natural parlance and made me a well-spoken anomaly among my street urchin mates, but it wasn't that. My lack of Cheetham Hill chat far preceded going to big school. It was the result of growing up in a house where such talk wasn't appreciated or accepted.

My dad was incredibly snobby about the way apna 'youth of today' would communicate. He saw it as an affront to hard-working parents who'd sacrificed everything to come over to this country for a better life – and more specifically a better life for their kids – only to have the new generation invent their own style of street speak that was a corruption of the formal English that was vaunted back home. I don't think that mentality is altogether uncommon among diaspora communities. It's the same way older gentlemen from places like South Asia and the Caribbean will take great pride in dressing very smartly in a suit and tie and polished shoes and lament kids in their communities for wearing low-slung jeans or shapeless T-shirts or even untucked shirts. It's perceived as not taking pride in yourself and not properly representing your community, even though the younger generation will take great care and pride in looking the way they do. I adore the old-school elegance of that elderly generation and think they look incredibly dashing, but a part of me wonders whether it's all mixed up with an imperial diktat about what's right and proper. Like a well-dressed residue of the British Empire.

Top 5 desi stereotypes that are actually true (Disclaimer: #notallAsians)

5) Arriving late: Some Asians are fastidiously punctual, and they should be applauded for their consideration and manners, but there are others (include myself) who are not always the most prompt. In fact, sometimes we could really do with a prompt to get going and avoid being late. Please understand it's nothing to do with anyone believing their time is any more or less important than anyone else's, it's just that we have a slightly more *elastic* concept of time. Never is this more evident than at Asian weddings, when the table of white work colleagues arrive an hour before everyone else, i.e. the time it says on the invitation.

4) Aggressive hospitality: This is by no means a bad thing – what could be more wholesome than treating a guest with utmost respect? But there's an intensity to Asian generosity which can be overwhelming to the uninitiated. More often than not it centres around food and offering one more samosa or pakora than you either need or want. Now that may sound like heaven to some, but you really need to understand the 'enough plus more' concept. If your limit is three, say two is enough and allow one more for negotiation. If five is your max, happily accept three and indulge an aggressively gracious host with the victory of two more.

3) Taking ages to leave: Again, it's that elastic time thing. In Asian culture, the declaration to leave and the actual act of leaving are distant relatives. And distant relatives are incidentally the worst culprits of the long goodbye. Imagine the scene: some inconsiderate guests have turned up on the day of a big match and you're desperate for them to leave before the 8 p.m. kick-off. After what seems like an eternity, your heart sings when they declare it's time to go at 7.30. Then begins the all-too-familiar charade of your parents saying 'No, stay,' your guests half-heartedly stating 'No, we really must go,' and then the soul-crushing overtures of a fresh new conversation when everyone's finally stood up. In such a scenario, you'll be lucky to catch the post-match interviews.

2) Parking/general road etiquette: This tends to be the preserve of a heavily-populated Asian area, usually around a busy desi superstore. You don't, for instance, get this problem with a few Asians at Ikea or a desi family at the Trafford Centre; it requires a critical mass of brown faces to somehow come to the collective agreement to ignore every road safety rule of the land. That includes parking and leaving the car unattended in the middle of the road, slowing down for impromptu chats with passers-by, deliberately veering onto the wrong side of the road to avoid the said parking and chatting, and pedestrians with a death wish sauntering in between moving vehicles like a bittersweet Richard Ashcroft.

1) Blunt questions: Very much a pet hate of mine but as inevitable as biting down on a bastard clove when eating rice. The main culprits are uncles and aunties – or more accurately 'uncles' and 'aunties' – who think nothing of asking the most personal and intrusive of questions of you in the most casually brazen fashion. They know they outrank you and leverage your respect by asking questions like why you aren't married yet, why you don't have children and how much you earn per annum. The only way to combat this is to fight fire with fire and innocently ask how their son's role as CEO of his own non-existent company is going. It won't be long before they say it's time to go, and leave an hour later.

Two affectations my dad especially disliked were filler words and the type of blasphemy that littered every casual proclamation with the name of God. The use of words like 'kasme', 'walla' and 'wallahi' just to add emphasis to a statement, like 'Kasme I just saw a pigeon come down and steal someone's food,' or 'Walla I'll slap you if you don't stop talking,' to essentially state 'I swear in the name of Allah' about the littlest thing was contemptible. To be fair I was on board with that and made sure not to mimic it even by accident. But I was constantly getting in trouble for using filler words. The ubiquitous 'innit' was a favourite along with 'wazagonnasay' and just loads of um's and er's. To this day, I have to stop myself saying 'like' and 'thingy' every second word. My dad would interrupt me, regardless of what I was saying, tell me off and make me very slowly and clearly repeat myself with no word clutter.

The problem was that it was part of my coping mechanism for having a stutter. It was pretty serious when I was little but gradually improved with time. So much so that I was eventually able to appear on the radio and podcasts and sound semi-coherent. If you'd have told me that back then I wouldn't have believed it was possible. I think I still have a very obvious stutter but there's a key difference: I used to be really self-conscious about it, and noticed it more than anyone else; now I'm cool with it and largely oblivious until someone mentions it; but never in a nasty way. As a kid, though, my stutter just drained all the confidence out of me. It was crippling in so many ways. I hated the constant fear of stumbling over my words and getting stuck on a particular word like a malfunctioning Speak & Spell. It was so bad that I'd often opt for not saying anything to save myself the embarrassment. And of course nerves made it worse. Elongating certain syllables and filling gaps with er's and erm's and thingy's helped with Charlie Chaplin, Harold Lloyd and Buster Keaton. Of course that was mixed in with more age-appropriate stuff like *Going Live*, *The Real Ghostbusters*, *Thundercats*, *Round the Twist*, *SM:TV*, *Home and Away* and *Neighbours*, but I was just as likely to quote Mel Brooks as Michelangelo (the turtle, not the artist; I wasn't a complete nerd). All that said, the one thing that offended my sensibilities like nothing else was when there was a cartoon on TV and you'd get excited only to discover it's some post-modern arty-farty animation from Eastern Europe about existential dread. Absolute bullshit.

Top 5 favourite 1990s movies

5) The Usual Suspects: At the time *The Usual Suspects* blew my tiny little mind. This was in the days before social media and everyone having the internet, and so a movie spoiler could remain a movie spoiler for months or even years. Obviously considering who was involved in the production, it is now more problematic than a Rubik's Cube with all the stickers peeled off, but I have to stay true to my younger self and include it in this list.

4) Trainspotting: I was obsessed with everything about *Trainspotting*. The music, the fashion, Begbie being a massive psycho, the cool as fuck editing, the creepy baby scene, the gross toilet, the poster (although I didn't *quite* go full student and buy one from HMV to adorn my wall). I did however buy the book of the script and Irvine Welsh's novel, which I adored and made very visible on the bus in the hope that it would make me look cool.

3) My Cousin Vinny: I love the likes of *Birdcage*, *Clueless*, *Grosse Pointe Blank* and *Swingers* (although I do wonder how well that one's aged), but I reckon *My Cousin Vinny* might be the best comedy of the decade. And one of the best ever. Pairing Joe Pesci and Marisa Tomei was such random casting and yet they are so perfect and hilarious together. No one else at the Cheetham Hill Blockbuster got a chance to rent this out because of me. Sorry about that.

2) GoodFellas: Obviously. It just about squeezes in because it came out in 1990, but there's a reason why everyone loves it and it's so incredibly hack to include it in this list. The scene in the bar where Robert De Niro clocks your man with the wig as Cream's 'Sunshine of Your Love' starts up is worth the entrance fee alone.

1) La Haine: It's a toss-up between *The Godfather*, *Sholay* and *La Haine* for my favourite ever film, and I think *La Haine* just edges it. Everything about it is perfect. The soundtrack is all killer no filler, the early

1990s sportswear chic is très magnifique, every scene somehow looks like both a documentary and a work of art, and the ending leaves you utterly numb. How can a film that is nothing about me, or where I'm from, speak to me about my life in such a profound way? 'L'important, c'est pas la chute, c'est l'atterrissage' is etched in my brain.

On occasions I would playfully be called a 'coconut' – i.e. brown on the outside, white on the inside – for some of my gorah hobbies. It wasn't ever done in a nasty way; just mates taking the piss out of each other. Although the definition of gorah as a descriptor for preferences/pursuits was so broad it sort of lost all meaning. For instance, nearly all my mates loved playing football at any opportunity, and would swear allegiance to a club. They'd claim to be a United fan or City fan or whatever, even if they weren't that into actually following a club. It was more for banter purposes, to rip the piss if your team lost or to claim your favourite player was rubbish. So vaguely following a club was fine, but doing it with any intensity – especially if you wanted to go to games – was seen as a bit gorah.

On the one hand there was a logic behind it, on the other it was almost self-fulfilling. Most of the faces you'd see at football games would be white, the whole culture around match days and congregating at a pub was white, so it was … white. But if it was therefore seen as a largely white pursuit, it would remain a largely white pursuit. A slightly less logical argument I had with a Muslim mate who supported Liverpool was that supporting Manchester United was un-Islamic, on account of the fact that the badge had a devil on it, or 'shaytan'. The same lad even went as far as grassing me up to the Imam once because I wore a devil-clad (Lindy Lou) United top in mosque. The Imam wasn't arsed and just remarked that I should dress smart at mosque and not wear a foot-ball shirt. We argued about it for a while (me and my mate, not me and the Imam) before I won by telling him to 'just shut up'. A few years later I took great delight in telling him his Liverpool shirt was 'haram' (forbidden) because it was sponsored by Carlsberg. A very late but very effective comeback, I'm sure you'll agree.

One of the weirdest anomalies growing up – and I think this is a pretty common thing among Muslim kids of that era – is that we were discouraged from even saying the word 'pig'. It was definitely a cultural thing rather than a religious one. As in obviously, swine of any kind is off the menu for Muslims as it is for Jews, but to not say the word?! Instead we'd go round referring to pigs as P-I-Gs – as if spelling the word out would technically circumvent some rule that didn't exist. It was used as an insult – 'You're a P-I-G!' – on those occasions when you wanted to slander someone but not go too far. I bring it up now because it was somehow okay to say 'the devil' or 'shay-tan', but 'pig' wasn't on. Even though the word is mentioned in the Qur'an more than once. Nowadays, people have thankfully realised it's absolutely fine to say it, as long as you're not chewing on the ham sandwich at the same time. Still, it's not as weird as racists and Islamophobes thinking that bacon is Muslim kryptonite and therefore leaving it on door handles at mosques and bizarre stuff like that. For the record, we don't recoil in fear or burn at the touch or even self-combust. You're thinking of vampires.

Even more than cavorting with whitey at the football, music was a major line in the sand in terms of how gorah or Asian I could claim to be. I was always into guitar music, which could broadly be described as 'independent' music, and later would briefly and naffly be rebranded as 'Britpop'. As previously mentioned, my first real love was the Smiths ... which is a lie really because it was actually Rick Astley. What I'll confess now that I refused to openly admit then is that the whole Stock Aitken Waterman scene was a massive guilty pleasure. 'I Should Be So Lucky', 'Never Gonna Give You Up', 'Especially for You', 'Too Many Broken Hearts', 'Together Forever', 'Love in the First Degree' – all absolute bangers then and now. I remember helping my older sisters record songs off the Top 40 rundown on Radio 1 and became adept at hitting pause just before the DJ came in to talk over the outro. I also used to read their copies of *Smash Hits*, and loved the fact they included the full lyrics of the biggest songs each week.

By the time I was around high school age I wouldn't dream of admitting to being a bubblegum pop fan because I was far too worried about being cool. It's a dumb phase that most of us go through during our teenage years when we pointlessly narrow our horizons in an attempt to appear credible. It's bullshit. Nothing's cool or uncool – you just love it or don't. I'd end up buying the likes of the *NME* and *Melody Maker* and make sure people saw me with them so they would know I was into 'proper' music. No one gave a shit; no one ever gives a shit. If they do, they're even sadder than you. Thankfully, that phase tends to pass and we eventually replace silly pretensions with honest pleasures. So I'll say it now and I'll say it proud: Rick Astley is ace. I was a bit too young for the Haçienda and the whole 'Madchester' scene, but much like the Smiths, I caught on to it late and with gusto. I was still at primary school when The Stone Roses and Spike Island happened – although judging from the number of Mancs who claim they were there, maybe I should pretend I was too, off my tits on ice lollies and double-popping lime and orange Tic Tacs. I was pre 'The Stone Roses by The Stone Roses', their début album, but well into it by the time 'Second Coming' came out, which admittedly doesn't narrow it down. I loved them, and Happy Mondays too. Like the Smiths, a big part of the attraction was that they were from Manchester (and Salford in Happy Mondays' case) but their music sounded so un-Mancunian/ Salfordian. It wasn't rainy and grey, it was sunshine and rainbows. The Stone Roses sounded really American to me, especially John Squire's guitar. It was like the Beach Boys or something. And for all the flak Ian Brown gets for his voice, I thought it was perfect for their sound. Years later I was at their big comeback gig at Heaton Park. It's one of the best gigs I've ever been to. There was something about the dizzy excitement among the fans that night that was electric. Everyone just beaming their biggest smiles like giddy kippers. I think for a lot of people there it must have been a magical little time travel to the best days of their lives. Music has the unique power to do that beyond any art form.

It's one of the things that people don't get about Oasis. There's always waves of changing sentiment about popular music that mean the very same band can be dismissed as lame and embarrassing one minute, and hugely relevant and celebrated the next. Take Phil Collins for example – at one point he was as lame as lame could be; the epitome of middle-of-the-road cocktail bar music. Now everyone loves him and he's even got a cult following among Zoomers oblivious to anything other than just digging his songs. At present, the prevailing narrative around Oasis is they're a bit 'yer da'. In the sense that it's seen as dated (for many it's their da's favourite band) and basic to like them; the whole 'just a shit Beatles' and 'the same three chords' stuff.

It totally misses the point. You didn't see them tearing it up at the Boardwalk and you didn't buzz off 'Shakermaker' being on ITV's *The Chart Show*, thinking 'this is class' even though it sounded just like that Coca-Cola advert. Oasis only make proper sense in the context of how they made people feel at the time. Certainly for me, they came at just the perfect time. I felt like 'Fucking hell. This is *my* band. I was too young to live through The Clash or The Jam or even The Stone Roses – but this is *my* version of that.' It was something massive that was happening right in front of us and dead exciting. You felt chuffed every time they were on the radio or telly, especially at the beginning. The music was great, but it was everything else too – the attitude, the Mancness, the way they dressed just like we did, the sense they weren't out to impress anyone. I could just about overlook the fact they were City fans, even if my inner monologue was massively Alf Garnett: 'They can support who they like behind closed doors, but I just wish they wouldn't shove it down my bloody throat!'

I must admit I got sucked into the whole Blur v Oasis thing, even though it was a load of nonsense. More than anything I was annoyed 'Roll With It' wasn't one of Oasis's best. It was like putting out a weakened side in a big game – you still want them to win but wonder why Mikaël Silvestre and Eric Djemba-Djemba are starting. Blur were alright, but they were a bit too nudge-nudge wink-wink for me. It's easy to be wise after the event but I think most fans of what could broadly be described as indie music at the time found the whole 'Britpop' label a bit cringe. Beyond the obvious fact it was a meaningless marketing gimmick, there was also the slight annoyance that everything you liked had gone mainstream. Suddenly everyone liked Oasis and it was like, well, you weren't arsed before but now you're a die-hard fan overnight?

In footballing speak, it felt like a load of glory-supporters had jumped on board. Childish, perhaps, but that's how it felt. My favourite bands of the era were Oasis, Suede, Gene (I went through an ill-advised side-parting phase to be like Martin Rossiter), Ash, The Divine Comedy, The Bluetones (who are criminally underrated to this day) and especially Pulp. *I* was the glory-supporter as far as Pulp were concerned. They'd been going for ages and yet I'd never paid any attention until 'Babies', and then obviously 'Common People'. Oasis meant more to me then but I think Pulp mean more to me now. 'Different Class' is exactly that. It's the finest album of that crassly named era – even above 'Definitely Maybe' – and the most perfect example of all-killer-no-filler. I adore Jarvis Cocker and he has replaced the hole in my heart left by Morrissey. He has all the wit, humour, kitchen sink sensibilities and ability to break your heart one minute and make you laugh the next – without causing your toes to fall off from fourth-degree cringe every time he opens his mouth.

Of course, my fondness of Britpop was the very definition of gorah music. I could argue until I was blue in the face that the likes of Cornershop, Saffron from Republica,

It's easy to forget the prominence of the Union Jack in the music scene of the time. Whether it was Noel's guitar, or Liam and Patsy Kensit's bedspread, or Geri Halliwell's dress, or even David Bowie and his Alexander McQueen coat. It was hard to avoid. And then there were all the magazine covers. To be fair to the acts at the centre of the cultural storm, they were powerless to stop *Select*, *The Face*, *Q* and all the rest from placing their likenesses in front of giant backdrops of red, white and blue. It was all ammunition for my mates to rib me by association. I was asked if I'd ever wear anything with the Union Jack on it. I said of course I wouldn't. It was an anathema to everything I held true: it symbolised British imperialism, the far right, a type of ugly and exclusionary nationalism that assumes superiority over others and treats foreigners as less than equals.

I would not wear that flag under any circumstance, regardless of how ironic or fashionable or reinvented or ubiquitous it may be. Other people could do whatever the hell they liked with it and good luck to them, but it just wasn't for me. Ever. I was asked if I was absolutely sure and I stressed in the strongest terms possible that it wasn't even up for debate. I was then asked to look down at my feet. I was wearing black Reeboks, with the tiniest little Union Jack next to the brand name logo on the side. Fuck. Betrayed by my own trainers. Damn Reebok and their surreptitious half a centimetre nationalism. Why couldn't they have used a little Lancastrian red rose to signify their

Bolton origins? It was good enough for Bolton Wanderers. I accepted my defeat badly and stormed off in a huff, my treacherous Reeboks mocking me with every step.

I wouldn't even mind, but the opposite of 'gorah music' was not 'apna (our) music'. If they were all massively into bhangra or whatever then, fair play, I'd be bang to rights, but they weren't so I wasn't. As far as I could tell, the opposite of gorah music was black music from America – and I was into that too. It was R'n'B stuff like Montell Jordan, Warren G, Shaggy, R Kelly, Usher, Bobby Brown, Coolio and Blackstreet, and hip hop like LL Cool J, Ice Cube, Ice-T, Snoop Dogg, 2Pac and The Notorious B.I.G. I liked some of that, but preferred De La Soul, Arrested Development, Fugees (we were all in agreement over them), Beastie Boys (more goreh), En Vogue, Salt-N-Pepa and TLC. TLC's 'CrazySexyCool' is up there with 'Different Class' for just banger after banger, albeit they were a lot crazier, sexier and cooler than a lanky guy from Sheffield.

In terms of hip-hop especially, a lot of my education and love for 1990s/early 2000s stuff came retrospectively. The likes of NWA, Public Enemy, Wu-Tang Clan, etc. It's important to remember that we were drip fed a lot of hip-hop that was massive at the time in the USA. It felt like a big deal when LL Cool J was on *Top of the Pops*, for example. So much so that I wasn't really aware of Jay-Z until 'Hard Knock Life' came out and it was like, whoa, who's this guy and how has he made a song from *Annie* sound so good. My mates were definitely ahead of me on the likes of Tupac and Biggie, and I definitely slept on Dr Dre. 'Nuthin' but a "G" Thang' was obviously a tune but it wasn't until Eminem burst on the scene, and then the release of '2001' that I realised how good he was and how many songs I loved that he'd produced. Anyway, the whole point of all of this is that my mates were giving me grief for buzzing off white music when they were buzzing off black music. Which now I've said it sounds like another win for them. But – again I stress – I liked hip-hop and R'n'B too, just perhaps a little less obsessively than indie music.

A massive influence on the music I listened to was the radio. A lot of people reference John Peel in introducing them to their favourite bands like The Undertones and The Smiths, but for me it was Mark and Lard. Or Mark Radcliffe and Marc Riley to be exact. I loved them. Everything about them. From their music to their daft catchphrases like 'Biggedy biggedy bong!' and 'Stop ... carry on!' They were so brilliantly funny together and so achingly cool, to me at least. I wanted to be their mate. The amount of late night hours I spent in my room listening to them prat about, play amazing new music and even champion great poets like Simon Armitage and Ian McMillan. A part of me died when they went to breakfast radio. Each night I'd either listen to them, or failing that, tune into local shock jock James Stannage insulting drunk people by calling them 'sad old donkeys' on Piccadilly 1152. I definitely didn't want to be *his* mate.

3) There Is a Light That Never Goes Out (The Smiths): A very obvious choice for a Smiths fan, but *what* a song. The chorus is romantic and twisted (in a very tongue-in-cheek way), while the verses are so full of doomed yearning. So many lines resonated with me, because I always felt I had so much to say but was ultimately too shy and unsure to say it.

2) Miss Sarajevo (Passengers ft. Luciano Pavarotti): I know what you're thinking: 'Bono, Noz? *Bono*?!' Well, first of all let me make it clear that I'm no great fan of the man, or indeed U2. But this song is the anomaly. It always made me cry and I didn't know why. I still don't know why. The lyrics would just hit me in a very profound way and of course Pavarotti's majestic vocals made it soar onto some other plane. The line 'Is there a time to turn to Mecca?' gave me chills. I found it so moving to have my religion referenced in such a lovely song.

1) Whatta Man (Salt-N-Pepa ft. En Vogue): You know how Carly Simon's 'You're So Vain' is both a searing indictment of male vanity but also so catchy and irresistible that men listening to it *do* actually think it's about them? Well, this is a bit like that but for the 1990s. 'Whatta Man' is clearly not about the likes of me. No one has ever looked at me and thought 'Whatta man!' But it's one of those songs that makes you feel, just for around four and a half minutes, that you could feasibly be that guy.

Top 5 favourite hip-hop tracks from the 1990s

5) Protect Ya Neck (Wu-Tang Clan): I've always loved the idea of a rap group and the way they all have their turn with their own individual styles; like it's a relay race and they're passing the baton to the next guy. The sound and look of the 'Protect Ya Neck' video is so gritty and raw. A part of you almost feels like you and your mates could grab a mic and have a go. I used to buzz off the fact that Inspectah Deck rhymed 'Pakistan' with 'Spider-Man', even though I was never quite sure what he meant.

4) Ready or Not (The Fugees): 'The Score' is easily one of the best albums of the decade and this is my favourite track. I loved the way the Fugees mixed up so many different genres like rap, soul, R'n'B and reggae into their own sound, and how that kind of mirrored their pride and representation of immigrants and refugees. 'Ready or Not' is so atmospheric and almost haunting, it transports you away to some other, far cooler place.

3) Still D.R.E. (Dr Dre ft. Snoop Dogg): Surely one of the best hip-hop beats ever produced, it always makes my hair stand on end whenever I hear that piano intro. Obviously, so much about what makes it great is Dre's production, but I think it's mad that Jay-Z wrote the lyrics for both Dre and Snoop's bits. To be able to mimic their respective styles and delivery, it's so perfect. In fact, I'd go as far as to say this Jay-Z character may have the chops to forge a career of his own.

2) Gangsta's Paradise (Coolio ft. LV): Everything about this song is so epic. From the Biblical first line to the choral accompaniment in the chorus, it all feels very religious. Coolio worrying about whether he would see out the year felt so chilling and poignant when I was a kid. That awareness and acceptance of your own mortality. And was some of the appeal that Michelle Pfeiffer appeared in the video as the world's most impossibly fit teacher? I guess we'll never know.

1) I Wish (Skee-Lo): Absolute tune. In the context of so many other rappers bragging about all their cars and women and wealth, I loved the self-deprecating humour of 'I Wish'. And obviously I could relate to the lyrics – I *too* wished I was a little bit taller (although I'd have settled for 5 ft 9).

Top 5 favourite indie songs from the 1990s (note: not necessarily Britpop)

5) Something for the Weekend (The Divine Comedy):
Neil Hannon is one of the greatest songwriters of his
generation. There, I said it. He's so witty and each song
feels like a play, they're so rich with character and plot.
'Something for the Weekend' is the pop version of *Dirty
Rotten Scoundrels* – a bounder gets his just desserts
when the woman he's trying to con turns the tables.
Sorry if that's a spoiler (or double spoiler), but it's been
30 years FFS.

4) Now My Heart Is Full (Morrissey): I can't be doing
with Morrissey these days. It turns out everything I loved
about him, he wasn't. I'd love to draw a line in his
discography between the Smiths stuff and his solo stuff
so I could use the oft-cited Johnny Marr disclaimer (i.e.
it's okay to like the Smiths' back catalogue because it
wasn't just Morrissey). But alas, I can't. I loved this song
– I still love it – as with numerous other Moz tunes.
'Now My Heart Is Full' encapsulated all the empathy
and feeling that Morrissey seems to have lost along the
way. I just can't explain, so I won't even try to.

3) Yes (McAlmont & Butler): A song that's so euphoric and uplifting that it ought to be prescribed by the NHS (note: at the time of writing we still had an NHS, *just*). What I love about 'Yes' is that as much as it's a joyous and spirit-soaring listen, the actual lyrics are so bitchy and full of sass. It's basically telling an ex that you've moved on and you're absolutely thriving without them.

2) Shakermaker (Oasis): Oasis aren't the greatest band ever and this isn't even their best song. But when I'm listening to Shakermaker at full blast, it feels like they are and this is. More than any other band in the 1990s, you can't separate Oasis from the time they were around and how they made people feel. This is the first Oasis song I ever heard and it was a revelation. I was so excited about this new band who felt like they were mine. I understand when people say Oasis are overrated, but I also understand when people say they were the best thing ever.

1) A Little Soul (Pulp): 'Different Class' is my favourite album of the 1990s. Every single tune is an absolute banger, with so much passion and feeling and wit and social commentary. It's a masterpiece of indie-pop. 'A Little Soul' isn't from 'Different Class'; it's from their next album 'This Is Hardcore', which is also brilliant but less boppy and much darker. I love the likes of 'Common People', 'Sorted for E's & Wizz' and 'Disco 2000', but I think this is Jarvis Cocker's saddest song and also his best. The lyrics are so personal and naked that it feels almost inappropriate to be listening in. It's a song that speaks to me in a way that is sometimes overwhelming and it always makes me cry.

While I was trying to perfect a razor-sharp side-parting, à la Martin Rossiter of Gene, and a nonchalant Liam Gallagher style swagger in my big green coat (I didn't have a parka so had to improvise with the padded winter coat we'd got from Uncle Manzoor), my Asian mates had two clear sartorial influences – Tupac Shakur and Will Smith. Even before his death, Tupac had a look that was iconic beyond his music. It also helped that he was good looking, had a six-pack, and could *almost* pass for South Asian if you squinted really hard. Plus he wore a nose stud that looked like a koka so he was practically Pakistani. As for Will Smith, he was at a stage in his career where he could do no wrong. He basically had everything: he was smart, he was funny, he was rich and famous, he was cool, he was good-looking, he was tall, he could do serious acting, he could do comedy, he could rap – all that and he was still in his mid-twenties passing for a savvy, wise-cracking West Philadelphia teen. *The Fresh Prince of Bel-Air* was massive in this country thanks to BBC Two showing it (and milking it for repeats), and of course everyone knew the intro rap off by heart. It was another example of Will Smith's range of abilities, in a Dennis Waterman style flex of writing the theme tune and indeed rapping the theme tune. Everyone wanted to be the Fresh Prince – including me. But to paraphrase a modern-day version of the rapper/comedian hybrid in Big Shaq, I didn't have the facilities for that, bruv.

Because he was my one link to school and Cheetham Hill, I hung around with Sajid a lot, and of the two of us, he was definitely the Will Smith. He was cooler, better-looking and wore nicer clothes. He was also more dangerous than me because he'd carry around a little lighter that he'd flick on and off. That made me his nerdier, squarer, less cool best friend. In short, it made me his Carlton. Many years later my sister introduced *The Fresh Prince of Bel-Air* to my nieces and nephews and they loved it. She asked them who Carlton reminded them of; they all laughed because they knew exactly who she meant.

It wasn't just Fresh Prince that made Will Smith such an attractive role-model. There was obviously his burgeoning music career, most notably his two big hits in the UK with 'Summertime' and 'Boom! Shake the Room' alongside his long-time friend and collaborator DJ Jazzy Jeff, and also his growing filmography – and one film in particular. I don't know what the cultural footprint of *Bad Boys* was like for the rest of the country, but round our way it was huge. Everything about it was adopted as some kind of aspirational blueprint for how to look, dress, sound, and exchange insults with your best mates. Again, Smith's Mike Lowrey was the one everyone wanted to be, while Martin Lawrence's Marcus Burnett was the consolation. Although I don't even think I was cool enough to be Lawrence. Incidentally, one key attribute that both Smith and Tupac shared, which was of massive appeal to young Asian lads at the time, was carefully trimmed facial hair. It was something to aim for with their own bum-fluff efforts.

As with music and fashion and various other things, films were another way in which I was veering away from my childhood pals to an increasing extent. Thanks to my eldest sister Ayesha, I'd got into what were slightly more independent films such as *The Commitments*, *Get Shorty*, *Shallow Grave*, *Reservoir Dogs* and *The Usual Suspects*. The last two especially were a revelation. I watched *Pulp Fiction* too and got a bit obsessed with Quentin Tarantino. Not only were they really cool and slick and full of loads of quotable dialogue, but the clever twists and obscure soundtracks made you feel smart for watching them. With my mates it got to be a literal fork in the road, where they'd want to go to the Odeon on Oxford Road and I started wanting to go to the Cornerhouse cinema. You've got to remember that I was going through a tragically pretentious stage, so if there was a film showing at both the Odeon and Cornerhouse, I'd want to see it at the Cornerhouse. I remember pleading with my mates to go and see *La Haine* with them because I knew they'd buzz off it, but they weren't having it because it was French and subtitled.

All this sounds like a hard and fast clash of cultures: me with my independent, pretentious 'white' tastes and my mates with their more black America influenced and mainstream tastes. It wasn't really like that. We enjoyed loads of stuff together and I had far more in common with them than I would ever have with anyone at high school. Most of our time together wasn't spent talking about films or discussing the Smiths, it was just enjoying each other's company doing whatever. Of course a huge element of that was playing football and (our concrete playground version of) cricket together. And – this might sound a bit weird – badminton too. Badminton was a big thing for us growing up. It was an affordable, convenient thing to get up to on a weekend. Rackets and shuttlecocks were cheap (ours were brought back from Pakistan) and Abraham Moss had courts we could play at. The funny thing looking back is we'd be playing wearing our normal clothes, like jeans or jumpers or shell suits. Even though badminton was dead knackering and we'd be sweating cobs, it never occurred to us to wear shorts or exercise appropriate gear. Some of our group smoked too so they'd be smoking between games, in the sports hall. And no one said anything. Simpler times.

After football and badminton, our favourite pastime by far was 'chilling'. We'd knock on and ask if you wanted to 'come for a chill'. It would mainly involve going to each other's houses, or hanging around and making each other laugh. Ideally it was the household most empty of parents and full of food. Having Sky Sports was a bonus but not essential. Sometimes chilling sessions took place outside, at a bus stop or a quiet road or near an old primary school. The important thing was the time and freedom to hang out with each other and dick about. And if you dared to come along wearing something new or you made the fatal mistake of mispronouncing something, you were the butt of the jokes for the next half an hour. That's the thing about mates – *real* mates – you can take the piss out of each other and you feel absolutely safe in doing so because (and I cringe while writing this) you love each other. You'd never dream of saying it to each other but it's true.

8.

HALAL! HALAL! WE ARE THE MUSLIM BOYS

I hate the term 'moderate Muslim' with an intense passion. That is to say, I hate it with a passion that is not moderate. The word 'moderate' can be defined as 'to (cause to) become less in size, strength, or force; to reduce something'. And the word 'Muslim' can be defined as a person who believes in and practises the religion of Islam. So what precisely does 'moderate Muslim' mean? That you're Muslim ... ish? That you're the inoffensive lemon and herb of Muslims? The korma and peshwari naan of the congregation? Does moderate Muslim mean you're not quite rated 18, but parental guidance is strongly advised?

It's a ridiculous term that wouldn't be used or make sense in any other context. Imagine telling a lifelong Manchester United fan who goes home and away through rain or shine that they're a 'moderate' supporter. Consider the nonsense of patting someone on the head for being a 'moderate' success in achieving or doing anything and expecting them to be grateful. I love you, moderately. I wish you all the best, within moderation. I really respect and admire how you've dedicated your whole life to a pious existence of love, light and spiritual betterment – but always only to a *moderate* extent. You never went *too* far on your journey to enlightenment, nor were you *that* arsed about becoming the best person you could be. For that you deserve my vindication. Well done, you moderately impressive person. Congratulations on being 'mid'. Have this cookie, because you're two-thirds of the way through fasting during Ramadan but that's fine because twenty is plenty when you're only moderately a Muslim.

Moderate Muslim goes hand in hand with that other virulent term, 'Muslim fundamentalist'. They're two sides of the same disparaging coin. It's like there's a sliding scale that goes from not at all Muslim to one hundred per cent Muslim, and you should never go full Muslim because then the Muslim-o-meter can't handle it and malfunctions. As terms go, I actually think moderate Muslim is worse than Muslim fundamentalist, because at least the latter is meant as a negative thing. There's no ambiguity about it. If someone describes you as a Muslim fundamentalist, you know it's not a term of endearment said with a handshake and a cheery smile. The reason why 'moderate Muslim' is worse is that it's used as if it's a virtue – or at the very least the lesser of two evils. It suggests an assimilation into polite, civilised society, as if you've been tamed of your more dangerous thoughts and instincts. It's the Muslim version of that backhanded insult that anyone from any minority has heard a variation of at some point or another: 'You're one of the good ones.' The bit that is (mostly) unsaid but strongly implied is 'I don't like your sort, but …' The common use of 'moderate Muslim' is the acceptance by a society that 'Muslim' without the 'moderate' isn't acceptable.

Eric Cantona nailed it when he pointed out that saying 'moderate' to describe a Muslim was wrong because it essentially framed Islam as an extremist religion. Eric called it 'latent provocation'. I get the 'you're alright for one of them' treatment quite a lot, and always have. I think it's because, for all my anti-social instincts and introvert inclinations, I can get on with most people. I also happen to sound more like Brian Cox than Babar Azam, so that helps. Essentially, if someone has never properly got to know a Muslim person, and instead has been fed everything they know about Muslims from the *Daily Mail* and the *Sun* and a whole plethora of TV dramas casting Muslims as either baddies or suppressed women, meeting me is going to be a revelation. Compared to some of their preconceptions of Muslims, I'm remarkably normal (and some would say boring). But that's less a reflection on me and more a reflection on what they've been made to believe.

Top 5 common fallacies about Muslims

5) Beards/headscarves equate to piety: There's an understandable assumption that outward displays of faith in terms of what people wear and how they present themselves are directly proportional to how 'religious' and practising they are of their faith. In my experience it's often a complete red herring or red hijab. There may be some level of correlation in certain instances, but some of the most committed and pious Muslims I know would not be immediately recognisable as Muslim if you passed them in the street. Conversely, some of the biggest beards and most tightly-wrapped scarves can hide a multitude of shenanigans. It's like assuming that a full-kit wanker at the game is somehow a more committed fan than someone who's wearing Stone Island (and getting the badge in).

4) Ramadan: Ramadan misconceptions could be a whole sub-section of their own. But as with so many questions asked of Muslims about our faith and way of life, you'll be amazed at how happy we are to clarify any misunderstandings or explain anything away – simply because it's so nice when someone takes an interest with an open heart. So, as a quick summary (deep breath): Yes, not even water; no, we don't die because we can eat and drink when the sun goes down; no, we honestly don't mind if you eat in front of us; yes, it is earlier this year (because our lunar calendar is shorter); no, just because a Muslim you know isn't fasting it doesn't make them bad – there's loads of caveats for people who don't have to or shouldn't fast. Ramadan is not just about fasting. It's a month of spiritual renewal and reaffirming the basic tenets of your faith.

3) All Muslims are Asian or Arab: This should be an obvious one, but it is remarkable how often the assumption is made (either consciously or unconsciously) that 'Muslim' equals South Asian or Middle Eastern. Islam is a religion that spans pretty much every culture and nationality in the world, and obviously that means that Muslims come in all shapes, colours and sizes. You could trip over a Muslim in any country in the world and not necessarily know that they're Muslim … unless you trip over them when they're praying in which case it would be pretty obvious. Trying to distil Muslim culture or appearance into one singular stereotype is like dropping a load of Mentos into a bottle of pop and immediately trying to chug it. You'll end up with a very red face.

2) Muslims hate Christmas: We don't hate Christmas, we're not trying to cancel Christmas, none of us are lobbying to change the name of Christmas (if you're annoyed at 'Happy Holidays' blame the Americans, not us) and we've certainly got no beef with Santa – a kindly man with a big beard who exercises the annual Muslim obligation of Zakat (almsgiving). This attempt to Grinch-ify the Muslim community is the sole preserve of weirdo Islamophobes who want to cause division and stoke the flames of hatred and 'otherness'. Personally, I love everything about Christmas, except for when they take one of my favourite songs and turn it into a slowed-down saccharine plinky-plonk cover version for a telly advert. Stop that.

1) Bacon: Bacon is not – I repeat NOT – a form of Kryptonite to be used against Muslims you don't like. We don't lose our superpowers if we go near it, nor does it burn our hands if we touch it like we're vampires or something (unless it's straight out of the frying pan). If you spend your precious time carefully placing uncooked rashers of bacon on the door handles of mosques in the dead of night, it's just a waste of your energy and good bacon. It would be just as inconvenient and gross if you used halal turkey rashers instead. In fact, I'll let you into a secret: what we *really* hate is KitKats. We're petrified of them. So if you want to intimidate or provoke us, leave a multipack of those please.

I wouldn't ever describe myself as a moderate Muslim. That's not because I think I'm a model Muslim – in fact I think of myself as anything but. I dearly wish I was a better Muslim than I currently am. If to err is human, I am incredibly, tragically, impossibly human. But I strive and hope and pray to become a better Muslim because my faith is so important to me. It's definitely not moderately important to me, or important to a limited extent. It's all-encompassing. In very literal terms, I am fundamentally a Muslim. In that being a Muslim is fundamental to who I am and who I try to be. It's more important than nationality, or culture, or money, or my career, or even football. It is the single biggest influence, aim and objective of my life.

That said, I am often surprised by how surprised other people are about how 'religious' I really am. I'm not talking about close friends or people who have known me for years and years, but people who kind of know me, through work and on a superficial level. On the occasions that my religious practices are apparent in front of them, usually around everyday things like fasting during Ramadan, or not answering a call because I was praying, or even just saying Bismillah under my breath before eating something, it can surprise them that I do observe my faith. Not in a bad way, it's just something they're not always expecting. I think most people realise that I'm Muslim early on, but don't necessarily know anything beyond that because why would they? It's not something I shout about or announce upon entering a room. It's most quickly evident around food or drink. The latter because I obviously don't drink alcohol, and the former because I'm a nightmare to be around when ordering at a restaurant. As well as having a number of annoying allergies including nuts, sesame seeds, crustaceans and molluscs (all this invariably means a separate 'allergy matrix' has to come out to supplement the standard menu), I also can't have pork or any other non-halal meat. But I will happily eat alongside someone who is putting away swine like there's no tomorrow and I will merrily meet friends in pubs and the like – I just won't partake in anything stronger than fizzy pop.

Actually, I tell a lie. One of my favourite things to do when I'm with my pal Jim – an expletive-loving Glaswegian who puts on a very convincing curmudgeon act when in fact he's one of the sweetest, loveliest guys I know – is to go into the dingiest, mankiest, least hospitable, feet-stick-to-the-floor pub we can find and politely ask whether they can do me a lovely strong cup of tea. Jim is always mortified that I would ask such a thing in his presence and even worse if they actually oblige. Speaking of which, I do get my round in and I accept that may not impress some people because I'm paying for other people to imbibe alcohol. But the way I look at it is a) my soft drink or cup of tea or whatever is always going to come at a premium at a pub/bar so it's cheeky to not pay my way, and b) part of what you're paying for is your table/seat at said establishment – the opportunity cost of someone else being there and spending more money than you on hard liquor – so paying for your round is partly paying to be somewhere with your pals.

For me, Islam is first and foremost a deeply personal thing and it always has been. I'm definitely not ashamed about my faith but don't feel the need to needlessly broadcast my religious endeavours either (he says, in a book called *Inshallah United*). Do you know that saying 'The empty vessel makes the loudest sound'? Well, invariably, the longest beard hides a multitude of sins. I mean that figuratively rather than literally – I don't want any ZZ Top fans coming after me. What I mean is, quite often the people who are loudest about judging others and commenting on how other people are living their lives aren't exactly paragons of virtue themselves. Growing up you'd see the occasional uncle sheepishly exiting the local Ladbrokes and then heading to the mosque. So what? It's none of my business if you're placing a cheeky wager on the 1.10 at Wincanton just before Friday prayer, but quite often the very same dude would be loudly condemning others – especially young people – for their un-Islamic behaviour. Leave those kids alone and go collect your winnings, uncle.

Personally, I just don't have the energy or inclination to go around telling others how to be better Muslims when I need to focus on my own failings in that respect. I'm not at the 'Islam? Completed it mate' stage to be judging others. I'm aware of how cringe this sounds, but I see

Islam as a light within me that I constantly need to nurture and maintain, and if I do that right, it will radiate out in good deeds and kind behaviour towards others. For me, it's something within that shines out, not the other way around.

Top 5 uses of the word 'Inshallah'

5) The true meaning: 'If God wills it' or 'God willing'. It's something that you say about any future event or circumstance that you hope will transpire. The rationale being that nothing happens without God's will and so you say a little prayer for that to be the case. It's so ingrained in common parlance that to *not* say it when verbalising a wish or a hope feels a bit like making yourself some fresh warm toast, throwing it to the ground and hoping it doesn't land butter-side down. If you don't say Inshallah in a room full of Muslims, they will instinctively and collectively offer one up like lighters at a Coldplay concert.

4) The ironic Inshallah: When someone says something so preposterous and unlikely that the Inshallah just emphasises how far-fetched the possibility of it actually happening is. As in, God willing this to happen is literally the *only* way it ever could, because all logic,

experience and good sense suggests the opposite.
Example: 'Yes, and Inshallah one day I could play in the
NBA in spite of the fact I'm shorter than Michael Owen
on my tiptoes ...'

3) The guilting Inshallah: Mums love this Inshallah. It
sounds like a sincere hope for your future endeavours,
but the context and tone of the Inshallah make it
abundantly clear that this is in fact a hollow Inshallah
designed specifically to make you feel bad about yourself.
This is the kind of Inshallah that Livia Soprano would
throw about like confetti. Example: 'I hope one day you
have children of your own who love and respect you
enough to call you once in a while, Inshallah ...'

2) The disclaimer Inshallah: This is very much the
sticking plaster of Inshallahs. Whether it's gossipy uncles
down at the mosque or a gaggle of aunties exchanging
hot news, this is the go-to Inshallah to take the edge off a
mean-spirited reference to a mutual's misfortune. It is as
if all manner of Lady Whistledown-esque snark can be
absolved with a religious afterthought. Example: 'Did
you hear about *her* carrying on with *him* and how they
both got what they deserved? Anyway, Inshallah
everything works out well for them.'

1) The never-never Inshallah: This Inshallah is a 'no', wrapped in a 'not likely', shrouded in a 'quite possibly'. Again, it is a favourite of the mums but certainly not their sole preserve. You learn to understand exactly what it means and resign yourself to the crushing of a dream. I suppose the closest translation for non-Muslim mums would be 'We'll see', which again means 'NO' in capital letters. If you ask for something as a kid and your mum says 'Inshallah' – or worse, the knockout combo of 'We'll see, Inshallah' – it's curtains. Just throw in the towel … unless it's a towel you asked for in which case you're not getting that either.

Islam is undoubtedly more important to me than football or Manchester United, but it certainly isn't separate to them. There's a definite overlap between being Muslim and a United fan. I don't see them as mutually exclusive aspects of my identity, but rather interconnected in a profound and important way. Islam imbues every single aspect of my life, from the most high-minded and noble ideal to the most trivial and banal detail. You may know that Muslims are meant to pray five times a day: Fajr (at dawn), Dhuhr (just after midday), Asr (in the afternoon), Maghrib (just after sunset) and Isha (at night). These prayers have set times (dependent on the length of the day), set durations (in terms of the number of cycles or 'rakat' you perform) and require specific ablutions to be done beforehand to ensure you are clean and in the correct mindset to pray. I would be a liar if I said I never miss a prayer, and I would be a bigger liar if I said there weren't times when I got lax in praying five times a day religiously. But I always try to and always feel happier and more fulfilled when I do.

The thing is, those five set prayers are not the beginning and end of praying for Muslims. As well as your prescribed five-a-day, you can also pray away to your heart's content at any other time. And I'm always praying. Mostly under my breath so as not to freak anyone out or, worse, seem like one of those Bluetooth wankers. I pray that I won't miss the train when I'm rushing to platform 14 at Piccadilly Station (located a cross-country run away from the rest of the platforms for some unnecessary reason); I pray they've got the Wallabee boot in my size at Clarks when they go to check in the back (and that the bored-looking staff member is actually looking); I even pray that the next Starburst née Opal Fruit will be a green one instead of a purple one because the former is the best and the latter is the worst (don't @ me). And of course, seeing as it's such a focal point in my life, I pray all the time about football.

The first time I remember being so invested in football that I felt compelled to pray for something to happen was during England's semi-final with West Germany at Italia '90. As previously mentioned I was completely and utterly swept up in that tournament, as the first World Cup I was old enough to properly appreciate. And obviously as a child you're so impressionable and take what you see and hear on telly and the radio so much to heart (this was of course in the days before the world wide web). The fact that England had started in such an underwhelming manner and then slowly grown into the tournament, finding form and a system that worked (and of course Paul Gascoigne) meant that there was a clear sense of, wow, something special is happening here. To use *X Factor* speak, England were on a 'journey'. They'd recovered from their version of their nan dying, i.e. a weak performance in the group stages and losing Bryan Robson to yet another tournament-ending injury, and they'd somehow made it to boot camp/the semi-finals. Witnessing all the hype around the game, and listening to people on TV talking about 'momentum' and 'destiny' and how 'maybe the wait is finally over', I was proper buzzing for the game and convinced that England were going to make it to the final. However, by the time 90 minutes were up I was a nervous wreck. I'd watched the last few minutes of normal time on mute, because my dad had put it on mute as it was time for him to pray. Usually he'd switch the TV off during prayer time so as not to be distracted, but seeing how absorbed I was and appreciating the importance of the game, he just put the sound down so I could carry on watching while he prayed. He finished just in time for the final whistle, which meant extra-time. If the 90 minutes was stressful, it was nothing compared to this added torture. I'd somehow gone from sitting on the sofa to being perched on the edge of the table. Wet with sweat and shaking with adrenaline, I found myself making wild involuntary movements with every kick of the ball.

West Germany had a few dangerous moments, with Peter Shilton making a really sharp save, but gradually England started to settle into the situation and looked like they were taking control. If anything, England were the ones trying to play efficient and composed football and the Germans were relying on passion and a big moment. Then what seemed like a nothing moment changed the whole mood. Gazza beat two men on the halfway line but looked like he was about to lose the ball to a third in Thomas Berthold. He went in for a desperate lunge and caught Berthold instead of the ball. The German went down like he'd just stood on a Lego brick and Gazza went to check if he was okay. I was just annoyed that West Germany had a free-kick and was oblivious to why Gazza was frantically doing the universal two palms in the air gesture for 'I'm innocent, boss'. Even when the referee ignored his protestations and pulled out his yellow card I was blithely unaware as to the repercussions.

By the time Gary Lineker had done his famous resigned look to the dugout and mouthed, 'Have a word with him,' the commentator had made the situation clear: Gazza would miss the final no matter what. Then I saw his little bottom lip come out like a little kid and his eyes well up and I did the same. I don't think I even properly got why I was so sad about it – in the back of my mind I knew they could always replace him with another player – but it's like when you're a child and you see another kid cry: your immediate instinct is to join in because they're obviously crying for a reason. Alas, there was no time to dwell too long on Gazza's misfortune because there was twenty more minutes of excruciating football to be played before you-know-what. Both teams hit the post – first Chris Waddle and then Guido Buchwald – and England even had the ball in the back of the net. Gazza was viciously chopped down by Andreas Brehme on the right flank in a manner that made you wonder whether he was trying to get a rise out of him to get him sent off. Waddle took the resulting free-kick and curled a lovely ball into the German box, which was met by a trademark David Platt header past Bodo Illgner. I jumped up in wild celebration but quickly realised it had been ruled offside. Curses! Not really understanding the offside rule at that age I just accepted it, but I've never understood why more wasn't made of it at the time or indeed since. It looked like a legit goal that could have secured England's place in the World Cup final and yet no one seemed arsed. Weird.

After what seemed like an eternity, Brazilian referee José Roberto Wright blew his whistle to signal the end of extra-time (while doing a funny little dance for dramatic effect) and the impending spectre of penalties. I'd been quietly praying for England to score for the last half hour but such was my desperation ahead of the dreaded shoot-out that I felt something a bit more substantial was required. With that I hurriedly grabbed the janamaz (prayer mat) and started praying in the direction of Mecca. An impromptu plea to God. Quite what my dad made of this I don't know. He'd never seen me so utterly possessed by football, or so passionate about anything for that matter. And he'd certainly not seen me whip out the janamaz like I was placing an urgent 999 call to heaven. Whatever he was thinking, he kept it to himself as I knelt before Allah and prayed my heart out that England would prevail from 12 yards. Admittedly one eye was on the telly screen to make sure I didn't miss the start of penalties, but just as dear old Bobby Robson was dishing out words of wisdom and organising who would take which spot-kick, and just like the physios were shaking cramp out of spent limbs, I too was doing my bit for the cause.

In praying for England to succeed and reach the final I was pushing the needle – however marginally – in their favour. And to start with, it felt like my efforts hadn't been in vain. Lineker, Beardsley and Platt finished with aplomb; it's just unfortunate that Brehme, Matthäus and Riedle did so too. There was nothing in it. You've got to remember this is before England had the well-earned reputation for being rubbish at penalties. There was no need to be afraid, especially with Stuart Pearce stepping up next. Pearce was famous for three things: his 'Psycho' nickname due to his 'uncompromising' tackling, the ridiculous size of his gargantuan thighs (eventually usurped in girth by fellow left-back Roberto Carlos), and his deadly free-kicks. He wasn't one to caress the ball into the top corner with the precision curl and dip of a Gheorghe Hagi or Roberto Baggio – his was more the traction engine thwack. Never mind the bollocks, here's Stuart Pearce. Of all the players who'd stepped up for England, I was most convinced that Pearce would score. His penalty would be low, hard and unstoppable. Alas, two out of three wasn't good. Illgner dived away from the ball but left his legs behind for insurance and Psycho was thwarted. As for Waddle, you could tell he was going to miss. He had the pre-emptively apologetic look of a best man who knows his speech is about to ruin a beautiful wedding and likely put nana Dotty in an early casket.

I was devastated. England v Argentina was already pencilled into my head, and now, well now it was an imperfect end to a perfect tournament. I was obsessed with Maradona, mainly due to his pre-match kick-ups and a World Cup binder I had which included that famous photo of him where it deceptively looks like he's taking on 37 Belgium players. I'd already been looking forward to England playing his Argentina. I'd seen countless replays of that dizzying goal and that handball. Fuelled by jingoistic media coverage, I saw it as a chance for revenge. I would even have been happy for Italy to have won it for the romance of it all, and the fact they had become and would remain one of my favourite teams (the silky blue kit, the even silkier Roberto Baggio, the anthem, Toto Schillaci's mad-eyed celebrations) but as it was it felt like a final between two baddies – again, largely fuelled by the prevailing narrative of the time. My dad could see how forlorn and close to tears I was after the penalties and offered the really unhelpful but well-intentioned 'It's only a game, beta …' And then after a few minutes of that not working, he said something that was extremely helpful, and out of character for someone largely confounded and often irritated by my over-obsession with football.

He told me he was proud of me for praying for something I cared so much about, and told me sometimes we don't get what we want because we're going to get something better in the future. I offered a teary nod of the head and felt a little bit better, even though I couldn't imagine what would be better than a World Cup. He went on to explain that no one's prayers are ignored, even if we don't get exactly what we want exactly when we want it. Usually I'd think, 'Oh great, we've just lost a game of football and now my dad's lecturing me,' but I hung onto every word because I was in need of some consolation. He went on to proffer that for all I knew there was a boy just like me who was praying for Germany to win. In a strange way that really did help. I imagined the German version of me, possibly with a mullet and stone-washed jeans, celebrating his country's victory with a heavily accented 'Alhamdulillah'. I felt happy for my imaginary Muslim doppelgänger, even if there was a lingering sense that his prayers had ultimately beaten my prayers on penalties.

Now I know that some people reading this will be rolling their eyes so far back into their disapproving skulls that they'll be able to see their own brains. I appreciate that as much as Islam and its teaching are fundamental to how I live my life, others will see it as pure hokum. They'll be annoyed at my dad for filling my impressionable little head with such silly notions and even more dismayed at the fact that I still – as a grown adult with some assumed level of basic reasoning and intelligence – hold on to such beliefs. And I know what they feel like screaming at me from the top of their lungs: 'THERE'S NO SUCH THING AS A GERMAN *YOU*!' You may think of me as a generally sensible chap with a massive blind spot when it comes to organised religion. Or less charitably you could dismiss me as a deluded and brainwashed simpleton. I get it and appreciate that point of view, but the thing is, I do genuinely believe in Islam. I believe with all my heart that there is no God but Allah and that Prophet Muhammad (ﷺ) is the messenger of God. If you think that essentially makes me an idiot and it's all a glorified fairy tale, that's fine. I don't mean to sound like one of these people who are so annoyingly magnanimous that it comes across as dismissive or patronising, but genuinely I can live with that opinion of me. I respect it in the same way I respect the fact that other properly sound people have faiths that by definition contradict my own.

The main thing is, what you believe shouldn't stop me believing what I want to believe and vice versa. Nor should anyone be forced to live a life they don't want to, or follow a religion they don't believe in. I don't mean it's okay to deny proven facts, but you can have a belief system around them. For instance, as already established, I pray about football all the time. As in the smallest of things. In between praying for world peace and long, happy, fulfilling lives for everyone I care for and love, I'll also pray that United get a late equaliser, or that they beat Chelsea to signing a particular player, or that a misfiring forward finally regains his form and proves the doubters wrong. The point is, I do that while also being aware that the manifestation of those prayers will be physical and earthly and dependent on practical things. When I was praying for Stuart Pearce to score his penalty, I wasn't expecting a giant hand from above to reach down and deviate the ball from its central trajectory; I just prayed that Pearce would kick it somewhere goal-bound that the goalkeeper wasn't. And if you don't believe that a Nottingham Forest full-back can be an instrument of the Divine, I can't help you.

If you were annoyed at my dad for comforting me with all that Muslamic mumbo jumbo, you're going to be screaming into your Ricky Gervais box set at this next bit. Because, in a revelation that will pique the interests of national and global security organisations everywhere, I attended a number of Muslim residential camps throughout the 1990s. That's right. Muslim. Residential. Camps. Before you consider hurriedly alerting the authorities, let me stress that none of them were anything like a Four Lions scenario. There was no bazooka missiles and a distinct lack of rubber dinghy rapids, although the latter sounds like fun. In the absence of proper family holidays either at home or abroad, what we *did* do as a family was stay a few nights in what was either basic student accommodation or a large hangar somewhere and fill the days listening to talks about Islam, mooching around Islamic stalls, eating halal food and taking part in sports and activities with other Muslim folk – all in a field or campus completely hired out by a national Muslim organisation like the Islamic Society of Britain or Young Muslims UK or their like. It was all above board and kosher (well halal) and nothing at all to worry about unless you had hay fever. Essentially, it was a bit like a Muslim Butlin's (I'm guessing because I've never been to Butlin's). I say 'as a family' but my dad always stayed behind because he couldn't afford to close the shop while we were away. That was a bit of a pity, but I think it was probably for the best. My dad would have been keen for us to 'make the most of it' by making it as educational as possible, whereas the thing that made it fun was the looseness and freedom. You could go to Islamic talks and workshops if you wanted to – and we did go to a fair few and they were great – but a lot of the time it was just about playing football or chilling out or going exploring around the site. For the camps where the accommodation was based in hangars, it was literally rows and rows of thin mattresses on the floor and you'd sleep on them in your own sleeping bags. I couldn't imagine my dad doing that. I also think he quite enjoyed having the time to himself at home. A bit of peace and quiet without five hyperactive kids knocking about.

As much as it was a family experience, the first time I went alone. It was during the summer holidays between first and second year at school and my first time away from home on my own. As we've already established my dad had no qualms about throwing us in at the deep end, and as much as I expressed my reticence about going away on my tod, my dad assured me it would be fine. My only frame of reference was mosque, which was strict and serious. There was a kind of no-nonsense approach to being able to read Qur'anic verses and knowing them off by heart. If you didn't know something or got it wrong, you were told off. I thought 'Islamic camp' would be like that. I wasn't convinced when my dad said it'd be fun and I'd enjoy it. That's exactly what he'd say if he wanted me to go to something that was decidedly un-fun.

My scepticism felt justified when my dad dropped me off with my oversized backpack at the local mosque. So this is the deal, I thought, it was a 'fun' camp at a Cheetham Hill mosque. But no, this was just the pick-up spot for the coach that would take us to the residential base. I can't quite remember where that year's camp was. I want to say Leicester, but I might be wrong. We literally spent the whole time within a university campus and stayed in student accommodation, so it could have been anywhere. I got talking to a couple of the lads on the coach on the way and they were really sound. I told them it was my first time away and that I was nervous and they said they'd look after me. Which was great up until we arrived and were told we were getting split up. I wanted to cry. They didn't want cliques based on where we were from so they were mixing everyone up. I was sharing a room with a Somalian boy from London called Abdi. He was a year older than me and around a foot taller. He was also a cocky so-and-so who didn't shut up. So basically the opposite of me in every way. Whereas I was shy, nervous and incredibly homesick, he seemed to be in his element, happy to be there and nonplussed about being away from home.

One of the first things he did while we were settling into our shared room was ask me where I was from. When I said Manchester, he said, 'No, where are you *from* from?' I said I was Pakistani and he looked at me and said, 'Nah, you ain't Pakistani, brother!' He explained that he had loads of Pakistani friends in North London and I was no Pakistani. Also my name, Nooruddean, definitely wasn't Pakistani. Who the hell is this guy to tell me I'm not what I am? It was rude and he was wrong. After a while of arguing that I was indeed of Pakistani origin, he essentially said we should agree to disagree and concluded I might be Algerian or Moroccan or something. All the time he had his head cocked with an annoying half-smile on his face, as if he was Columbo or someone interrogating me and I was about to be busted. When I retaliated by questioning where he was from, he answered he was Somalian from North London. Before I had a chance to question the validity of that answer, he asked me what football team I supported. I answered Manchester United and he burst out laughing. I was raging. I was already on the verge of tears because I was homesick and now I was ready to cry out of anger. Who was this guy and what was his problem?

'Why? Who do you support then?' I shot back, mainly to stop his stupid laugher. 'I'm an Arsenal fan, bro!' he replied, with a big beaming grin on his face. Arsenal had just won the league comfortably – their second in three years – and it looked like they might have finally broken Liverpool's decades-long stranglehold on English football. From my point of view it was literally the worst answer he could have given – I was hoping for Spurs or maybe Chelsea. He definitely had the upper hand on bragging rights. United hadn't even finished in the top 5. Things were definitely looking up with two cups in two years, but realistically we were miles off challenging for the title. That said, we did absolutely hammer Arsenal 6–2 at Highbury in the Rumbelows Cup in one of those freak performances where everything goes right. I listened to the game with my sister Usmaa on the radio and we sat there absolutely buzzing and incredulous at what was happening. Arsenal were unbeaten and massive favourites so we'd have been ecstatic to scrape an undeserved win. As it was we thrashed them, Danny Wallace and Lee Sharpe – who scored a wonderful hat-trick – tearing their miserly defence to shreds. Me and my sister just got giddier and giddier after every goal. Not that any of that was much use against this Abdi character. All I could muster was a pitiful 'Yeah, well, Lee Sharpe. We beat you 6–2!' It was water off a duck's back. I think he was still laughing from before.

As much as he did my head in on that first meeting, we started to get along. I don't know whether he was emotionally mature beyond his years or it was just a by-product of his incredibly open personality, but his ribbing and non-stop chat actually helped me get over my longing for home. He just wouldn't let me pine or disappear into myself. There was a communal kitchen area where we'd make our own cereal before a leader dude would come in and take us on activities. Abdi introduced me to everyone and said I was his brother Noor-ud-dean, pronouncing every syllable in its correct Arabic intonation. I asked him if he already knew everyone he was introducing me to and he said he didn't. I wished I had half his easy confidence to just speak with confidence and authority like that. I saw him a few times here and there during the day, but we ended up having proper long chats about football once we retired to our room at the end of each day. He was Arsenal mad and said David Rocastle, Michael Thomas and Anders Limpar were his favourite players. He even had a legit replica shirt – yellow with black sleeves and a black JVC sponsor (the one before the famous 'bruised banana').

Being daft lads we argued over who'd win in a fight between United players and Arsenal players, a debate that was born of the fact both clubs were involved in a 'brawl' at Old Trafford a month before the 6–2. It was nothing really, just a load of shoving that lasted about 20 seconds after Nigel Winterburn tried to go in hard on Denis Irwin and Irwin retaliated. But the FA massively overreacted and docked us one point and Arsenal two points (because they had previous). Anyway, the point is United would win a fight easily because Mark Hughes, Bryan Robson and Gary Pallister would batter everyone and Les Sealey was unhinged. Obviously Abdi had a thing or ten to say about that. Another memory I have of Abdi and that camp involves Macaulay Culkin. It was raining on one of the days and we were scheduled to play football, but it was a washout, so we ended up watching *Home Alone* on VHS on one of those tellys on a stand with wheels. I don't know if it was an official copy or a knock-off but it was the only film handy so it had to do. The funny thing was, the fella supervising us didn't realise *Home Alone* was a Christmas movie, and panicked at every reference – as if he'd get letters of complaint off angry parents or something. Any time the C-word was mentioned he paused and explained we Muslims don't believe in Christmas and told us a fact about Eid. When we got to the part where Kevin visits a church with Old Man Marley, he sat himself down and started fast-forwarding the film. Abdi and I started booing at the back and got told off. Then everyone started booing and your man caved to public opinion and let us watch it – church choir and all. To the best of my knowledge none of us converted to Christianity off the back of that viewing.

It was the days before mobile phones or emails or anything like that, so at the end of camp Abdi and I said our goodbyes and promised we'd see each other at a future camp. Of course, life being the rich and random tapestry that it is, we never met again. But I'd remember him whenever Arsenal were on ITV's *The Match* or there was an Anders Limpar poster in *Shoot*, and I even developed a weird soft spot for the Gunners for a very short while because of him. I suppose that's the nature of these things – whether it's a family holiday to Benidorm or an Islamic camp in the East Midlands – you meet people, are best friends for a few days and that's it. Each time we went to one of these Islamic camps it was different, but always great. We went to one in Malvern, and one in Nottingham, and I think one in Wales too. As well as all the activities and talks, it was a great way of meeting people from different cultures and different parts of the country, and the only thing you'd have in common was being Muslim. I think it's hugely important that non-Muslims realise that Muslims come in all sorts of shapes and sizes, and vastly different cultures and backgrounds. We're not all Pakistani or Arab or whatever. But I also think it's just as important that Muslims themselves are aware of that. Islam does not belong to any one culture, and it's always good to remember that and see that in action.

I've found supporting United similar to that. One singular commonality can be the glue that bonds people from vastly different worlds together in a really profound way. Another thing I loved about those camps was not feeling like you were in the minority for once. It was great to do Islamic things and openly enact my faith without it seeming odd – or even threatening – to someone else. Even just to hear the gorgeous sound of the Adhan calling us to prayer and not worrying about who might take offence or get angry about their country 'being taken over' was nice. You could argue I could have got that feeling in Pakistan, but even there I wasn't quite one of them. I was Angrezi, or English. At those Islamic camps I was around people pretty much just like me – Muslims living in the UK – whether they were Pakistani, Malaysian, Cockney or Somali. It was novel and a lovely change. But alas it was not real life, and I was always overjoyed to come back home to Manchester and to my other people – Mancs. It is infinitely better to be a minority in the real world than to build your own world because you're a minority. It just *is* – even if a reminder of your roots and spiritual centre is important. Being Muslim around non-Muslim people who love and respect you for it is the best, and I mean that in the most fundamental way.

Top 5 non-Halal things I've always been intrigued by

5) Pork scratchings: So it's bits of pigskin that have been deep-fried until they're hard and crunchy, and then they're salted and sold in little packets like crisps? I mean, it's obviously not my halal bag, but each to his own. A greater issue/concern for me is the matter of porcine follicles. You can occasionally get *hairy* scratchings? And that's *fine*? You don't immediately throw it away, and then throw the whole packet away? And then burn down the pub you were in? Call me old-fashioned, but I like all my food to be balder than Pep Guardiola.

4) Wine: I love the way wine is described. It's completely mad. The more people describe it, the less sense it makes. There's notes of this and there's notes of that: woodiness, fruitiness, earthiness and even cheekiness. I've even heard wine referred to as witty! Tells jokes, does it? In my head, red and white wine taste like red and white grape juice, or Shloer – which is clearly not the case because apparently it's often not sweet and sometimes even a bit vinegary. Sorry but that sounds rank.

3) Getting extremely drunk: I like to be in control. To the extent that I feel a tiny bit annoyed when I'm given a nice surprise. That's my problem and I know I've got to deal with it. But it makes the idea of getting so drunk that you're not fully cognitive quite scary to me. I don't mean that drunk people scare me (unless it's a hen do) – I mean the idea of *me* being that drunk would freak me out. Or maybe it wouldn't, because I'd be drunk. But when people say they can't fully remember the night before because they were absolutely wasted, I panic on their behalf. How did you get home? Does some sort of internal sat-nav kick in? Either way, it's kind of impressive/frightening.

2) Bacon and gin: Why is everyone so obsessed with these things? I get it – people love things and like talking about them. But how good can bacon be? I've had turkey 'bacon' and that's quite nice (although I appreciate it's hardly the same thing), but surely the hype that bacon gets is a bit much? It's nice but massively overrated, like Coldplay or Jack Grealish? And gin, why is that suddenly a thing? It's as if around five years ago, gin got an amazing new agent and PR department and now it's cleaning up at all the awards ceremonies while rum pretends to clap and be happy while silently fuming inside.

1) Guinness: There are so many alcoholic drinks that I have neither the desire nor inclination to ever actually try but am fascinated by nonetheless. Baileys and anything that's the colour blue, for example. But Guinness is the one that piques my interest the most. I always ask about it and I always get a different response. It tastes a bit coffee-ish; it's iron-y (whatever that means); there's a metallic quality to it; it has the consistency of milkshake but the taste of Supermalt; it turns your shit into black tar. Then there's the fact that it apparently tastes completely different depending on where you drink it, whether that's Dublin, London or Lagos. A teetotaller asking about Guinness is like walking into a wardrobe and ending up in a very dark and gloopy Narnia. Still, great adverts.

9.

(SONG FOR) MY STRETFORD END SISTER

Growing up with three sisters and a brother in a flat that clearly wasn't designed for three girls, two boys, a mum and a dad was not without its challenges. We were always on top of each other and doing each other's heads in. The abundance of Choudrys and lack of room meant three things were always at a premium – peace, privacy and hot water. Funnily enough they were all interconnected, seeing as the only place to collect your thoughts without interruption was the bathroom. Even then, any moment of zen would soon be shattered by an aggressive bang of the door for you to get out and let the next one in. Failure to vacate the one private chamber in the flat would soon be followed by the three words most used among us five little shits. 'I'm gonna tell!' was the nuclear option that was used every five minutes. It meant pestering mum or dad (nearly always mum) about how Razi, Ghazali, Usmaa, Ayesha or

Saadia was doing you wrong by doing something you were doing to them just a short while earlier.

I look back and wonder how the hell my mum kept her composure in the midst of such whiny little grasses. It's not like she didn't have enough to do without playing UN to a bunch of squabbling siblings who loved nothing better than to get each other into trouble. The reason why Mum was always the first option is because it would be a short, sharp shock – one or both of you would immediately get an earful and that'd be that. With Dad there was always the risk that the next couple of hours could be a complete write-off as he'd invariably sit you down, explain that your arguments were the result of too much spare time and explain how you needed to do something more productive with your time. It just wasn't worth the risk of having your life-choices questioned at the age of 12.

To add to the sense of being crammed in together like too many samosas in a Tupperware box, our family transport situation was even more claustrophobic than the flat. My dad owned the same car throughout my childhood and it was clearly something of a hangover from his devil-may-care days sans Choudry brood. It was a black Ford Capri. For the seven of us. I don't want us to sound like the punchline of a 'How many Pakistanis can you fit into a _____' gag, but the answer is far too many. I know very little about cars but it had an 'S' on the side so I'm guessing it was a model S. It certainly wasn't S for 'spacious' because even four people would have been a tight squeeze. Getting into it via one of the two doors while folding back the front seats was an act of contortion in itself even as a kid. I've seen it described as a 'two-plus-two coupe', which is generous because as far as I could tell it was made for two smallish adults and maybe a couple of those handbag-sized dogs in the back.

I've also seen it described as 'the car you've always promised yourself' in the Ford marketing blurb of the time and that's probably more accurate. I guess it was one vestige of my dad's youth that he didn't want to give up. Suffice to say family outings involved a lot of sitting on each other's laps. I'd always get allocated my brother, which was the bum deal of the lot, and I mean that literally. Not because he was particularly heavy or cumbersome – I would gladly have welcomed some extra padding – but because he had the sharpest arse in the world. His bum bones were like elbows digging hard into my thighs. I'd end up with dead legs from the slightest bump or movement. It wasn't however the most discomfort I experienced in that car. That occurred when I had the backseat all to myself while suffering an anaphylactic attack after accidentally eating peanuts. My dad was rushing me to A&E as my throat swelled up, triggering my asthma. He was so stressed that he was smoking like a chimney – with all the windows rolled up. Thankfully, we reached the hospital just before I was hotboxed to death in a black Ford Capri. What a way to go.

Part of the reason we were always in each other's faces is that we were on our own. Beyond a handful of relatives in Glasgow and London, we were half the world away from anyone else. There were no relatives about to pop around to or to take us off our parents' hands for just a solitary afternoon. It was the seven of us on top of each other's heads in one flat above a fruit shop and no one else. We were also alone in terms of neighbours. The closest residential roads were near my primary school. As a child, I'd watch soaps like *Corrie* and *Brookside* and dream of living in a normal street (or close) with real-life neighbours, because, in the velvety croon of Barry Crocker, everybody needs good neighbours. I also yearned to live in a normal house with an upstairs and downstairs, and fantasised about yelling 'IT'S NOT FAIR!' to my mum and dad before running upstairs to my bedroom and slamming the door behind me.

Alas such things – a humble terraced house, a bedroom of my own, an overachieving cousin I could be unfavourably compared to – were but mere pipe dreams. We didn't have a garden, just a concrete yard. My brother Razi and I used to invent our own truncated sports and rules to play there. For instance, our version of a boundary in yard cricket was literally hitting the opposite wall – and a six was if the ball then bounced all the way back to hit the wall directly behind you. Any ball games risked losing the ball to either the roof of our flat on one side or the road below (over the gate) on the other. My brother (the budding Mowgli that he was) had developed a method of getting onto the roof to retrieve the ball via a leg up onto an adjoining wall, but it was fraught with danger. Not of falling off but our dad hearing his footsteps on the wafer-thin ceiling. Such were the obstacles to having a good time while living above a shopping precinct.

That said, the one advantage we had was the precinct itself. Cheetham Parade was a square surrounded on all sides by shops, including a fruit shop (directly below us), a health food shop, a carpet shop, our dad's hi-fi store (Zenith International), Cordon Bleu (a little mini mart), Pandora's Box (a haberdashery), a newsagent, a betting shop and a few more assorted units. There was also a greasy spoon cafe that stood in the middle of the precinct. The precinct itself was all drab concrete, apart from a bench area where old nans sat under huge cherry blossom trees. In spring/summer, they were almost surreal in their incongruous beauty – a grey asphalt space, surrounded by cold glass shop frontage on all sides, and then this huge cacophony of colour from the gorgeous pink blossom. Like something out of Japan, if you ignored the overcast weather, strewn Quavers packets and occasional white dogshit. In its heyday, the precinct was the bustling heart of the community, with plenty of footfall, mooching about and general chatter. But on Sundays it was pretty much deserted. And that meant us Choudry kids had it to ourselves – with provisos.

Unless we were using those extremely soft spongy balls from the little cheapo toy corner of the local newsagents, any sort of ball games were out of the question; breaking one of the shop windows was unthinkable in terms of cost and the amount of trouble it would get us into. Even setting off a shop alarm wasn't worth the repercussions. But we could at least run around a lot, have races and a game of tig. The bench area was a natural 'den' for the latter pursuit, while the greasy spoon was great for chasing someone vigorously around it in one direction and then suddenly running the opposite way and scaring the crap out of them once they'd turned the corner straight into your path. For a while we had a second-hand Raleigh Chopper, which was great fun to ride around in circles again and again and again. The fun of this was a) feeling a sense of blissful freedom with the cool wind blowing in your hair, and b) knowing that the next sibling is impatiently waiting for their turn and getting increasingly pissed off because you're taking way too long with yours. As any child knows, half the joy of playing with something is the knowledge that another kid wants it and will have to bloody wait. I bet a young Pep Guardiola was unbearable in that respect, never giving up possession of his Rubik's Cube even though he'd completed it four times.

As siblings, we'd bicker all the time and in every possible combination. Ayesha and Usmaa would argue because they were so close in age and so different in personality;

Razi and I would fall out every time we played anything with each other about who'd actually won; Saadia would always want to be involved and get away with whatever because she was the youngest. For some reason Ayesha and I had joint custody over a Walkman so we'd constantly row over that (and who was always draining the batteries); Saadia and Usmaa once had a full-blown argument over the word 'parasite', which Saadia used as an insult against Usmaa's friend without understanding what it meant; Razi and Saadia would get up to mischief together and blame one another over the fallout, and I once went into a prolonged mood with *everyone* when my gold Coca-Cola yo-yo – not Fanta, not 7Up, not even regular Coca-Cola – but my *gold* Coca-Cola yo-yo went missing and no one had the decency to own up to it. I still have my strong suspicions, and naming no names, maybe this book will lead the guilty party to finally admit it was him.

It's funny, though, how things change as you get older. There's so many variables to life, so many ups and downs, that you begin to really cherish the constants and grow closer to those who have been through it all with you. As much as we annoyed the living hell out of each other when growing up, time has a funny way of putting a different perspective on those tumultuous days at the flat. I've always been close to my brother from day dot. My parents never tired of telling me – usually after an argument with Razi – that it was my birthday wish to have a younger brother, and then he arrived two days before I turned

piss a bit. I think the vital thing that bonds the five of us in particular is that shared experience of living a life that only we know. All those moments of great joy and intense sadness, magnified by the fact we were second-generation immigrants living this strange, new hybrid experience of east and west combined, Muslim and Manc, British and Asian – and even more so by the fact we had no extended family within a 160-mile radius or even a neighbour within five minutes' walking distance.

We probably talk as much now as we ever have, albeit via the WhatsApp family chat. And personally I find so much to admire in each and every one of them. Ayesha for her immense kindness and gentle nature; Razi for his charming outgoing personality and strong faith and spirituality; and Saadia for her resilience and resolute optimism even through the toughest of times. They all have qualities that I know I lack. I think Usmaa is probably the most and least similar to me. We both have the same wicked sense of humour and very similar tastes, but whereas I'll overthink things and doubt myself, she'll just do it. Rather than express her derision by silently brooding and holding a lifetime grudge like I'm prone to do, she'll fizzle and pop in anger and then all will be forgotten. And whereas people often mistake me for being generous and good-natured when I'm not really, she doesn't always receive that kudos when she actually is.

I hate to say it but I sort of hero-worshipped Usmaa when growing up. It's not like I thought she was great or wanted to *be* her. As I said, we always had very similar tastes and I suppose she always got to things first on account of being three years older. Perhaps a better way of describing it is she was extremely influential in shaping my opinion on things. If she said a famous person was rubbish, it would put me off them; if she said Converse All Star baseball boots were in, I took that for granted (and if the next week she said they were suddenly lame and Doc Martens were the way to go, I'd happily follow suit). By far the two aspects of my life she was most influential in developing into fully formed passions were music and football. Without her, I may never have deviated away from mainstream chart music to more indie predilections or gorah music.

I very much doubt I'd have become so enamoured by four scrawny white boys posing outside Salford Lads Club with guitars and gladioli without her steer. Football was slightly different because I was always destined to surrender an unhealthy part of my existence to that, but she was my constant companion and ally in following the Reds. I may not have inherited an allegiance from my forefathers or had the standard parental guidance in adopting a club, but I did have a partner in crime who provided some much-needed support and validation when I was chastised for caring too much for a sport that would never love me back. Whereas my relationship with football has remained consistent throughout the years – to the extent that as a grown adult I am often dismayed at how much I still give so much of a shit – Usmaa's interest has boomeranged. She was mad into it, then lost a bit of interest, and now she's back with a vengeance. When we were kids she was probably more obsessed than me, and very much the driving force behind doing something about it. She used to write questionnaires to players addressed to their clubs – often random players like Dave Beasant and Ray Wilkins – and get really well-thought-out replies back. She'd take me with her to the old Cliff training ground in Higher Broughton (probably under the pretence we were going to the library or something) and we'd snatch some glimpses of Alex Ferguson and Archie Knox putting the United players through their paces without any jobsworth security telling us to sod off.

I hate to be one of those bores who claims we had it better in the old days and modern football is rubbish, but it's true. I used to watch the excellent James Richardson on *Football Italia* and would marvel at how Italy had so many newspapers, television programmes and even whole channels devoted to football. It seemed utopian to have such a wealth of football coverage, especially compared to the relative scraps we were feeding off in this country. Such was my eagerness to consume as much football content as humanly possible that I couldn't envisage there ever being enough, never mind too much. That was before the internet age of course, which is a bit like being locked in a room with nothing but five thousand cigarettes and a plastic lighter. I guess it's a case of careful what you wish for, because there's a lot of perks to being a bit niche that disappear forever once you pass the saturation point. It's when lucrative demographics replace committed hobbyists, and mass consumption takes precedence over human connection. Goodbye Higher Broughton, hello secluded and super-secure Carrington.

I remember when Usmaa took me to a local game of cricket down the road. I was at the peak of my interest in the sport thanks to Wasim Akram and Waqar Younis, but was very confused as to why Usmaa had suddenly shown an interest for the first time in her life. That was up until I realised who was playing – it was a 'Bryan Robson Celebrity XI' versus the 'Cheetham Hill Cricket Club Entertainers XI'. Bryan Robson – in Cheetham Hill! I couldn't believe it and was of course buzzing to go. My sister had got the tip-off from one of her mates that it was a charity match in aid of the 'Mend a Broken Wing Appeal' at Royal Manchester Children's Hospital and would feature an array of local footballers and well-known celebrities. I was happy those poorly kids would benefit from my £4 admission fee, but to be perfectly honest I was far more focused on who would be there.

It turned out to be the most surreal day of my tiny little life. Like one of those dreams where everything is super realistic and believable except for certain details like the dog can talk or your dad is Gordon Burns off *The Krypton Factor*. Not only were there a plethora of United and City players within touching distance, but they were all donned in cricket whites and acting very merry indeed. I read somewhere once that as strict as Fergie was in terms of curbing the drinking culture at United and using his network of spies to ensure no one was out partying too late, he made an exception for charity events and so the players would take full advantage. A favourite night out for Fergie himself was an evening of bawdy humour and camp cabaret at Foo Foo's Palace on Dale Street, where legendary Mancunian drag queen Foo Foo Lammar would entertain the manager and his players and raise many thousands of pounds for the Christie Hospital in the process. We were a little young and innocent for that scene but the players were taking full advantage of the free bar at Cheetham Hill Cricket Club.

There were two types of players on show: those taking the game extremely seriously and those having far too much fun in the pavilion to care. No one was going too far, they were just well-lubricated, relaxed and really charming and friendly to those of us who'd come to gawp at our heroes. As well as Robson, there was Lee Sharpe, Gary Pallister, Steve Bruce, Brain McClair and Clayton Blackmore, and City's Paul Walsh, Fitzroy Simpson, David Rocastle and Peter Beagrie, among others. Pallister, Robson, Simpson and Rocastle were especially nice. They were all happy to sign autographs and chat away. We saw Rocastle after the game about to get into his car and he was ever so patient and lovely. As for the 'celebrities', they were a bit wasted on me. It was mostly soap stars I didn't know because I didn't really watch *Corrie* and the like, but I did recognise Mike Le Vell, Phil Middlemiss and Sean Wilson who again were very generous with their time. One member of the celebrities team I certainly didn't know at the time was one of the biggest legends there – former Lancashire and India cricket captain Farokh Engineer. Despite my ignorance he was an absolute gent and I'll always have a massive soft spot for him in my heart. A big part of the day was collecting as many autographs as possible. I did my best but was a bit shy to ask. At one point Engineer – possibly sensing my bashful hesitancy – grabbed my programme off me and handed it around to get his teammates to sign it. What a lovely guy.

Celebrity cricket aside, the most cherished memories I have of growing up as a football fan alongside my sister revolve around the 1992/93 season, when the famous Manchester United finally won the league title after 26 long years of trying. It was the first season of the newly founded Premier League and the first to be broadcast on Sky Sports. There was loads of hype around it, including an expensive advert featuring the likes of Vinny Jones, Darren Anderton, Gordon Strachan, Peter Reid and Bruce Grobbelaar and soundtracked by Simple Minds' rousing 'Alive and Kicking'. I wasn't sure what it all meant or how exactly it was 'a whole new ball game', but what I did know is that it was the end of ITV's *The Match* and that was a terrible blow. No more live games on terrestrial television meant no more live games for us, because my dad wouldn't countenance us having satellite telly.

It was partly a cost issue but he also shared a very common snobbery at the time towards visible satellite dishes on the side of houses. It was perceived as a bit 'council house' – which from our point of view was a bit rich considering people in council houses were better off than us. There was also the feeling that anyone requiring any more than the four standard terrestrial channels was a square-eyed couch potato with an unhealthy obsession with the lowest form of entertainment. It was nonsense of course, but that was certainly a popular sentiment at the time. Sajid *did* have satellite television and so it was incredibly exciting to pop over to his to watch the odd game, for a sneak peek behind the forbidden curtain at this shiny new Sky Sports business. As much as I resented the fact they'd stolen football and Elton Welsby from my telly, if I'm honest I was a bit bedazzled by all the ritz and glitz on show. These days I'm utterly dismayed at the slightest attempt at Americanising the game, but back in the day anything remotely American was aspirational and just incredibly cool. When for example a McDonald's opened in Cheetham Hill, it felt like a Hollywood film set had landed in north Manchester; from the golden arches to the toadstool seats, it was all so glamorous. Similarly, Sky Sports shamelessly mimicking US-style sports coverage was really overblown and incongruous in a pretty exciting way. The colours were so over-saturated and gaudy and the graphics such a brutal attack on the senses – even the presenters were shouting at you for no apparent reason. But I loved it.

Unfortunately, my exposure to this bright new world was all too rare. In the absence of televised games, I took to relying on the only two realistic alternatives: radio and teletext. It was of course no consolation to watching the game on television (and obviously didn't compare to being at a game) but it's a testament to the power of the human imagination to fill in the gaps that both listening to commentary with crowd noise and literally watching slides of score lines on rotation could be thrilling in their own way. Not that it was new to us. Even in the halcyon days of First Division football on terrestrial you were only talking one televised game a week, and so the numbers 140 (Oracle), 302 (Ceefax), 1152 (Piccadilly Gold), 95.1 (Greater Manchester Radio) and 693 and 909 (Radio 5) were permanently branded on the inside of my brain.

Teletext was a bit like *Soccer Saturday*, but instead of the likes of Charlie Nicholas, Matt Le Tissier, Phil Thompson and Alan McInally explaining breaking scores, you had them quietly showing up on a screen – in other words better than *Soccer Saturday*. At its best it was thrilling. It was usually a full list of simultaneous fixtures that didn't fit on one page, so it would start by showing one page of two and then the other. But as the goals started to appear with a list of goal-scorers (and any sendings off) they'd have to use an extra page, so it was one of three. On particularly goal-heavy days it would be one of four pages, and that meant a longer wait to see your team's page pop up. The number of times I'd be watching teletext with minutes to go for United to score a vital equaliser or late winner – quietly praying under my breath all the while – and hey presto, United's page would appear with an added 'McClair 87' or 'Hughes 90+2'. I'd punch the air and give out a quiet 'Alhamdulillah' at the late intervention. Teletext also had the added non-football use of makeshift censorship too. If you were watching an age-appropriate film with Mum or Dad in the room and there was a random bit of naughty business going on, you could quickly press the teletext button (and mute if necessary) and wait for it to be over instead of dying of embarrassment.

As for football on the radio, it's no exaggeration to say it was the soundtrack of my adolescence beyond any particular band or music artist. I'm no flag-shagging nationalist, but I do think there are certain art forms and industries in which the UK surpasses itself. The film industry – with the likes of Shane Meadows, Ben Wheatley, Warp Films, Danny Boyle, Ken Loach, etc. – is one; music is obviously another; and the quality and depth of the UK's current (not just legacy) comedy scene is, I think, world-class. As for radio, it is something that we do as good as anyone, arguably better than anywhere. You only have to consider how incredibly popular the BBC World Service is to appreciate the standing in which it is held. Of course the BBC are a big part of that, and I'd go as far as to say that radio output is the jewel in their crown. But the quality of independent and pirate radio is also exceptional. Some of my most treasured memories of experiencing football, outside of actually being there, have been listening to the radio rather than watching on TV. There is an intimacy and an urgency to radio commentary that television cannot and could not replicate. TV obviously has the all-important visuals, but that very fact means the talk around the action is by its very nature supplementary and sometimes superfluous. With radio, there's an absolute need to explain everything – the action, the context, the mood and the fallout.

The greatest broadcasters do it so wonderfully. I remember listening to Cantona's kung-fu kick against Crystal Palace unfold in real-time and it was utterly thrilling. I couldn't believe what was being relayed and didn't dare imagine what the ramifications would be. And as ever, Usmaa was by my side to experience it with me. It sounds quaint to say it now, but there was nothing better than huddling around the radio, often with hot cocoa if it was cold and the gas bottle heater on if it was freezing, and listening to United on the radio together. For the majority of that historic 1992/93 season, that's exactly how we experienced it. One of the good things about experiencing it as a pair is that we cancelled each other out – or at least Usmaa cancelled out my constant doom. If she was glass half full, I was the glass smashed to smithereens in a puddle on the floor. I was constantly fearing the worst, whereas Usmaa was forever hopeful before the event and positive after it.

Having said that, there were plenty of moments of dread considering it was a title-winning campaign. Still scarred from the previous season, we started like an over-stuffed Ford Capri in reverse. We'd already suffered a blow in the summer when Southampton's Alan Shearer, a player who seemed destined to join us, went to Blackburn Rovers instead. Our consolation prize was Dion Dublin from Cambridge United. By the time the first table came out (after the regulation three games) we were 20th, having lost two and drawn one. And just as Dublin looked like he might be the player to spark our goal-shy attack, the poor guy went and broke his leg. It looked like we'd regressed badly and that the previous season had been our best chance to win that elusive title. In fact, it was only Giggs who looked like he was in any kind of form. Then of course the whole world turned on its axis with the surprise signing of Eric Cantona from Leeds. We were hovering between 8th and 10th when Eric signed and didn't really look back from that moment on. I was quite excited when the news broke because he was known for being a flair – if perhaps not decisive – player and his brilliant hat-trick in the Charity Shield against Liverpool was still fresh in the mind. If nothing else he'd be fun to watch.

Of course, being the relentless font of misery that I am, I never imagined he'd be the catalyst for everything else that followed. Usmaa, being the giddy kipper that she is, proclaimed he was exactly what we needed. She even wrote to him for an autograph. I said he was a famously mardy Frenchman who would never reply in a million years (of course I was wrong and he most graciously did). Even after the King found his spiritual castle there were ups and downs to the title run-in, and we experienced it all in technicolour radio. The lows felt hopeless – losing to Ipswich at the end of January and going on a devastating four-game winless run in March that left us in third. But the highs were beyond euphoric. Absolutely destroying Norwich with counter-attack after sensational counter-attack to end our March woes, and of course that amazing, chaotic, barmy game at Sheffield Wednesday. I was so desperate for us to get something out of that game I was close to tears. For once I didn't argue with Usmaa that it was a lost cause, because I was clinging onto her fierce optimism for dear life. She was right and I couldn't believe it. That night I thought to myself I really love my football-mad sister. But I love Stephen Roger Bruce more.

That was the day we went top and stayed there. Oldham Athletic – who I've always had a little soft spot for – did us a lovely favour at Villa Park and the title was finally ours. Even winning the league was enhanced by the humble wireless. We made our way to Old Trafford and enjoyed the festivities outside, hoovering up all the news-papers for posterity. Through a combination of the fans' singing and hearing them again and again on the radio,

(SONG FOR) MY STRETFORD END SISTER

Tina Turner's *Simply The Best* and Queen's *We Are The Champions* turned into the ubiquitous ear worms I never wanted to lose. So synonymous are those two songs for me with that moment in time that any subsequent use of them by any other club feels like shameless plagiarism. One of my favourite memories of that title win isn't the raucous celebrations at Old Trafford, or even the frankly Biblical (Qur'anic?) scenes in town for the open-top bus parade – it's silently colouring in homemade signs with my sister while listening to a Piccadilly Gold compilation show relaying the biggest moments of the season. I don't know if they still do it, probably not, but it was such a good idea at the time. Listening to dramatic commentary of the most vital goals without the slightest bit of stress or fear. I remember we bought the cassette tape of it too, so I could listen to it again and again on the 135 or 52 bus. It never ceased to give me chills, and I'd always say 'Alhamdulillah' repeatedly after every retrospective equaliser/winner.

It's great to experience special moments like that alone, but it's always better with someone else – be they family, friends or loved ones. I've noticed that with my nieces and nephews. They're a really lovely, sweet, intelligent, funny and kind bunch of kids who (Mashallah) get on like a house on fire and (Inshallah) always will. It makes me so happy that they have the extended family and constant house-hopping we never had when growing up. Maryam, Abdulhameed, Saleem, Ali, Sara, Eesa, Zain and Sophia are all Red to a greater or lesser extent – there was a bit of concern that Ali might plump for Burnley (from his dad's side) but we brought him back from that particular fate.

Ali, Zain and Saleem are the three that are most into football at present, and going with them to games has renewed my excitement for it all over again. It never went away really, but as already established my natural disposition can make me veer towards the negative and almost resent how much I love football. The nieces and nephews have definitely made me enjoy it again. They have the optimism for United and the unquenchable/daft hope that I've always needed to do away with my needless pessimism. As a kid it was Usmaa and now it's them. And because we're now the adults and in charge, they get to go whenever they want and get season tickets and watch football on telly every day of the week if they so please. But as much as that is great and gratifying, there's a lot to be said for the rationed output we experienced as kids. It had its own charm and kind of magic that I don't think I'd swap for any amount of high-definition Richard Keys.

10.

WASIM AKRAM 1 NORMAN TEBBIT 0

There's a lot of talk these days about divisive 'culture wars' and how the modern political landscape is now forever bifurcated, probably due to Brexit or something. What Alan Partridge would call a 'scissored isle'. But if you look hard enough, it's always been there – this tribal instinct that simplifies the world into being like football. You wouldn't support both Manchester United *and* Liverpool, would you? No, so what's with the dual passport? There just seems to be an innate facet of the human psyche that requires an emphatic and final answer.

It is something that is never more apparent and acute than in matters of nationality and patriotism – that double-edged sword of ultimate division. It's either one thing or the other; you're either with us or you can fuck off back to where you think you're from. And that's just if they're polite enough to give you the option first. In a way, it's almost simpler for first-generation immigrants. There is no doubt they have it tougher in every single possible way, but they're put in a bracket whether they like it or not. And by way of a natural defence mechanism, they can try extra hard to appease and fit in. But the real problems start with these second-generation ingrates. Not only do they simultaneously steal all our jobs and live a life of leisure off our benefits, but they have the temerity to be ambiguous about their allegiances. Or worse still, they're supporting the *other* side?! Enoch Powell didn't die for this!

In 1991, Norman Tebbit crystallised this sentiment in an interview with the *Los Angeles Times*. In case you're not familiar with Tebbit, he was Margaret Thatcher's arse-kisser in chief, and resembled an angry, bruised testicle that had just been sat on. He still does, albeit more shrivelled and with slightly greyer pubes. In this infamous interview, he used cricket as a way of stoking up racial tensions that didn't require any added help. He pointedly questioned why it was that members of immigrant communities who had settled in England persisted in supporting the international cricket teams of their origin, rather than England. His exact words were: 'A large proportion of Britain's Asian population fail to pass the cricket test. Which side do they cheer for? It's an interesting test. Are you still harking back to where you came from or where you are?'

It wasn't so much 'dog whistle' as a very loud foghorn. The kind of question you let hang in the air like a silent-but-deadly fart and wait for like-minded bigots to get a whiff and accept as their own. It was as much a reference to West Indies supporters living in the country as it was Pakistan or India fans, and definitely tinged with a level of bitterness that England were regularly handed their arse by those very teams. I wonder if any interviewer at the time had the gumption to ask Tebbit what his opinion was of English people abroad, in places like Gibraltar or Benidorm or Hong Kong or working in the Middle East, who remain fervent England football fans despite there being footballing nations far closer to their adopted homes? Or maybe it was just cricket – a sport that was readily exported to every corner of the Commonwealth to make up for all the theft and pillaging and invading and massacres and slavery and concentration camps and culture wiping and famine and 'displacement' and ethnic cleansing and bloody partition that was knowingly under-taken in the name of the British fucking Empire – that Tebbit was particularly arsed about? Maybe that was it.

Of course the Empire played a significant role in peoples from former colonies maintaining a sporting allegiance to 'back home' – even if the legacy of imperial rule wasn't at the forefront of everyone's minds when Malcolm Marshall or Imran Khan was running in to bowl. We were only here in the first place because of Empire; if it wasn't for the 1948 British Nationality Act and this country's very selfish and urgent need to address its severe post-war labour shortage with cheap and willing labour, we'd still be where we were, picking up the pieces from all that theft and pillaging and invading and ... you get the picture. As it was, we (I'm using the collective 'we' one generation removed) were here and being made to feel like second-class citizens because we *were* second-class citizens. That sense of feeling inferior to white people was drummed into us (again, collective, once removed) for generations both as children of the Empire and newly minted citizens of the metropole. Its residue still infects the minds of people of colour everywhere, from wanting straighter hair and thinner noses to making Fair & Lovely's skin-lightening cream bring in over £250 million in revenue on an annual basis.

It still makes me feel sad when I see grainy old footage of immigrants from places like Pakistan and India setting foot on British soil for the first time, or arriving from the Caribbean on *Empire Windrush*. Not because they look fearful or impoverished or weary in any way, but the very opposite. They look immaculate, with their starched white shirts, perfect Windsor knots, polished brogues and smart trilby hats. You can see the twinkle of hope and possibility in their eyes at having finally arrived in a land they've built up in their heads from everything they've learnt at school, and read, seen or heard about in their own corners of the great Empire. Living in a social construct, where everything that is right and proper and moral is a direct reference to how things are done in this almost mythical land on the other side of the world, must have conditioned them to believe they'd arrived at the centre of the universe. The reason those images make me so sad is because they have no idea what lies ahead – the racism, the struggle for acceptance, the slow dying of that young, vibrant light within them. They look so eager to fit in and embrace their new British identity. If I think about it too much it makes me so angry. Little did some of those beautiful young faces know that they'd be forcibly deported in their dotage thanks to an ungrateful and inhumane Tory government and their 'hostile environment' policy.

I think it's sometimes easy to forget just how recent that sepia-tinted past really is. It is just a generation ago. It's not my great great grandparents. I've not had to go on *Who Do You Think You Are?* to find out about the struggles of my ancestors via some kindly librarian wearing white gloves. That's my mum and dad. That's what it's like for a whole generation like me who were the first to be born over here. Some of that baggage is bound to carry over in all sorts of ways. You can live in a country and a time where chicken tikka masala is accepted as the national dish and held up in parliament as a shining beacon of 'modern multicultural Britain', and yet be stupidly embarrassed when your white friend from school comes round and the house smells of your mum's delicious homemade cooking, that he'll lap up with unbridled glee. You can have the most beautiful and inspiring name, like Nooruddean, and bastardise it to a shortened version for Caucasian tongues that sounds less like a heavenly title bestowed by God and more like a replacement part from B&Q for your garden hose.

As you get older and wiser, you (hopefully) embrace what makes you different and celebrate your own unique culture, but it's a personal journey we all need to go through and it's not always easy. What helps massively is if you've got people who look like you, and have a few of the same circumstances as you, doing big things in the world. As someone from a particular minority, you can find yourself grasping for *any* reflection of yourself in wider society just to feel that connection. I'm sure you've heard that cliché of someone from an ethnic minority household urgently calling the rest of the family to the living room because there's someone on the telly who looks like them. It's only a cliché because it's so true. We all did it. Whether it was Lenny Henry on *New Faces*, Madhur Jaffrey cooking chana daal on BBC Two, or Ken Hom with his trusty wok, it was a buzz to see just a flash of representation anywhere. And it always meant more on proper TV or in an English newspaper, rather than say in a Bollywood film or the *Daily Jang*, because you knew white people would see it too. It was mainstream, not just for you. It's so important to feel as if you're part of the greater conversation and the wider culture. And if you see someone who looks a bit like you succeeding in a particular endeavour or field, it can begin to feel almost possible for you. It validates you and gives you the confidence to be more yourself, safe in the knowledge it needn't be a barrier to entry or disqualify you from achieving your goals. And of course it gives you someone to follow.

I sometimes wonder what it would have been like to have an Asian football role model growing up. How would that feel? How amazing would it be? To have a brown footballer to look up to and maybe even aspire to emulate. When the hype started around the 'Class of '92' – winning the FA Youth Cup against Crystal Palace in 1992; losing in the subsequent final against Leeds in 1993; one-by-one making a name for themselves in the first team – I felt a huge sense of pride and emotional investment in them. Of course there tends to be collective soft spot among fans for players who've graduated through the youth academy rather than been bought for millions with no prior affiliation with the club, but for me it wasn't really that. They were older than me for a start, so I wasn't going easy on the kids. For me it was more that a lot of them were local. I'd read all about the Busby Babes (having a deep and slightly morbid fascination with them) in the books I'd borrowed from the library and ones I'd bought for a pittance at jumble sales. I knew that a fair few of them were local lads too: captain Roger Byrne was from Gorton; Eddie Colman from Ordsall; Geoff Bent from Pendleton. Survivors Albert Scanlon and Dennis Violett were from Hulme and Fallowfield respectively, while Wilf McGuinness was from Collyhurst way. It felt like a bygone era when players just lived in the terraced streets near Old Trafford and walked there on matchday.

generation who were actually good enough. You always need one breakthrough, one representative who makes it feel possible for everyone else. For me, it would have done wonders just for my pride in myself. It's not like I was ever apologetic or embarrassed about who I was, but at an age when you're desperate to just fit in you do get insecure about how you're perceived by others, especially if how you look or sound isn't conventionally cool or widely understood. That's why I was so internally embarrassed when I noticed a Pakistani tinge in my accent after I came home from Sahiwal and went straight into a new school; because suddenly it seemed as if I might be a foreigner rather than someone who lives a 135 bus ride away. A version of Nooruddean Choudry playing for United – or any club for that matter – would have been lionised and looked up to by me of course, but it would have mattered just as much if my white mates were idolising them too. I know such a yearning for external validation sounds desperately needy in an adult context, but as a kid it did matter.

Here's an even sadder version of that: I remember a few of us went over to my mate Anil's house (Anil was a lovely lad from Bury Grammar and my only proper brown friend at school apart from Sajid) and we spotted a poster of Bollywood actress Madhuri Dixit on his bedroom wall. One of our white friends – I think it was David – asked who it was. When Anil told him, he replied, 'Oh right, she's gorgeous' – and I was actually a bit chuffed that he found an Asian person attractive. Like I was secondary flattered by the fact that this teenage lad from Rochdale happened to find one of the most beautiful women in the world attractive. How messed up is that?!

In the absence of a football role model of an Asian persuasion, I had to look elsewhere and find the next best thing. One of the big Pakistani heroes of my childhood wasn't even Pakistani. Prince Naseem Hamed looked apna, dressed apna, moved apna, and even had an apna-style high fade of the like you only got at Asian barbers where they spelt 'haircuts' with a K and a Z. He could easily have been from Cheetham Hill, albeit with the thickest of Sheffield accents. He seemed so apna you could've sworn he had a few Bally Sagoo tapes in his car that he'd bought from Pan Rhythm on Wilmslow Road. Alas he wasn't apna at all – he was Arab, of Yemeni descent. But in the absence of a Karachi Kanchelskis or a Lahori Lee Sharpe, there were enough similarities between him and me for the dream to be real. We could definitely have passed for first cousins, if not brothers. We were both short; both Muslim and brown; both working-class and Northern; both proud owners of what could be described as a 'Roman nose' (via Sahiwal and Sana'a); and importantly we were both southpaws (although granted I used mine to continually draw that pointy 'S' in school exercise books, not for fighting). Even 'Noz' and 'Naz' were close enough to satisfy the Asian urge to name kids as a sing-songy pair.

The one thing Naz had that I didn't was the part of him that I admired the most: fearlessness. He just did not give a shit. In any immigrant community, the first wave are naturally the most cautious and inhibited, and subsequent generations have the luxury to feel more settled and confident about who they are. Naz had skipped around 12 generations and arrived from a future time where cultural insecurity just wasn't a thing. It was like he was so head over heels in love with himself that your opinion, good or bad, was incidental. You could either jump aboard his magic carpet ride of self-generated hype and leopard-print bombast or you could fuck off. There was no compromising or diluting to taste. The fact that he walked into the ring (before Cirque du Soleil-ing over the ropes like Jackie Chan on springs) with the Union Jack and Yemeni tricolour side-by-side was a big 'oof' in itself, but the brazen confidence to recite the Shahada in front of a sold-out arena full of well-lubricated boxing fans – in *America* of all places – was beyond anything I'd ever imagined. To me and many Asian lads like me, he was a revelation. We claimed him as our own in an act of brazen appropriation that Vanilla Ice would have been proud of.

It was interesting to see how the media reacted to both his showmanship outside the ring and his flair within it. Hamed's chin-out hands-by-his-sides stance, the way he would break out the Ali shuffle at any opportunity, and his full-on rhythmic gyrating (as if getting down to his own silent disco) didn't exactly endear him to sections of the boxing fraternity. Words like 'outrageous' and even 'scandalous' were used in the media. A lot of it was a natural aversion to taking the piss. Sport in general and sports journalists in particular have the strangest relationship with athletes enjoying themselves or putting on a performance for their fans. It is frowned upon as 'disrespectful' to the opposition if you pull off an audacious piece of skill just for the hell of it. The fact Prince Naseem was such an outrageous and consistent showboater that he'd put all of Nick Kyrgios, Ronaldinho and Ronnie O'Sullivan to shame was obviously going rub certain commentators up the wrong way, but there always seemed to be an extra little edge to their irritation. It was like they were desperate for him to get his comeuppance and be taken down a peg or ten with a good crack to the jaw.

I get that his style was bound to annoy some people, but for those of us who'd had it drummed into us from a young age to keep our heads down, not make waves, not upset anyone, always be grateful, never to rock the boat or draw attention and *always* remain faultlessly humble, well ... it was great to see Naz lording it over all comers. He refused to be anyone's pet anything and we loved him for it. He could so easily have said all the right things, pleased all the right people and toned down his essential Prince Naseem Hamed-ness. Perhaps then he'd have won the BBC Sports Personality of the Year award he so clearly deserved and gained the approval of *Daily Mail* readers everywhere as 'one of the good ones'. He could have played the good immigrant and received a grateful pat on the head. As it was, he didn't and they couldn't pat him if they tried – he'd just effortlessly bob out of the way and blow a petulant kiss.

It wasn't just that Hamed was a dancer either. He could punch too – hard. It was always fascinating to me seeing the two fighters in the ring square up. Hamed was obviously in impeccable shape, but he was nearly always smaller-looking than his opposite number. His legs and arms would always look stringier and less defined, and his shoulders scrawnier. But no amount of bulging biceps and pitbull-style traps could deal with Hamed's speed and power. If it was just a case of Hamed ducking and diving and essentially running away from a fight until his rival was spent, that would be one thing. They could grumble about how they'd have laid him out if only they could catch him. But it was the fact that he had the power in those green bean arms to knock them the fuck out. They weren't flailing at a crisp packet in the air, they were facing a lethal weapon. Seeing as us Asians aren't always the biggest, it was a buzz to know that our short king and adopted brother could do either fight or flight with the same contemptuous ease.

It's a completely different scenario of course, but the disconnect between mass and hardness in football was similarly fascinating. Take Roy Keane. He was clearly taller and bulkier than Naz, but by no means 'big' compared to a lot of his peers. And yet he was renowned as a hard man who rarely came out second best in any crunching encounter. Then you had the likes of Nicky Butt and David Batty – neither boasting a frame or physical presence of any great threat, but they were as tough and menacing as anyone. Even little Dennis Wise could more than handle himself. As much as all these aggy white boys were sources of inspiration for short arses with attitude (SWA) such as myself, to have a little brown Muslim lad with a buzzcut able to generate enough power to spark out much bigger foes was particularly appealing. Did it somehow make me harder by association? No. Did it inspire me to hit the gym and emulate my leopard-print clad brethren? Also no. But it allowed me and many others like me to take vicarious pleasure in someone smashing the easy target stereotype. Maybe that's a little part of why some people had such an impulsive aversion to him.

Talking about an aversion to people, let's get back to Snoreman Tebbit and his daft little test. My first memories of cricket are mostly as wallpaper noise. When I was very young, I remember my mum ironing a huge jumble of clothes in the living room, with a Pakistan cricket match on in the background. Barring the occasion piques of interest, she didn't even seem to be watching – which kind of made sense to me because half the time it was just writing on the screen, and most of the other half was people standing about and pointing. I don't know if she was multitasking or whether it was a relaxing form of proto

ASMR. All that speaking in hushed tones and polite clapping. In any case, it certainly didn't appeal to me. I just wanted to watch cartoons, not men dressed in all white doing nothing much but occasionally taking a few steps towards and prodding the ground with their bat (in later years, playing our own version in the yard, my brother and I would routinely – and in all seriousness – prod at the concrete floor as if getting rid of any divots).

The first time I properly got engrossed with cricket wasn't until 1992, with the far more colourful and action-packed one-day version. It was the ICC Cricket World Cup final between England and Pakistan in Melbourne – and I didn't even know the tournament was on. I'd stayed up to watch Des Lynam tell me about England v Czechoslovakia on *Sportsnight*, but they were showing highlights of the cricket too. I'd unintentionally managed to succeed where Likely Lads Terry Collier and Bob Ferris had failed and so didn't know the result. My dad interrupted me watching it by saying 'Watch this, beta,' pointing to the screen I was already glued to. It was as novel as it was superfluous. 'Watch this, beta' was usually reserved for something boring and educational, not sport. In hindsight my dad obviously knew the result but I was oblivious.

If it was England against any other country, I would have been supporting England. But it was such an exciting development to have a Pakistan team in the final of anything that I was compelled to support them. It's something Tebbit would never understand; that natural yearning to be excited about a part of you that you don't often get to be excited about. For context, the only times Pakistan and sport ever mixed in my universe was occasionally finding out we'd done okay in the hockey, the odd snippet about Jahangir Khan's latest squash victory, and celebrating when Pakistan appeared in the Olympics opening ceremony. But Pakistan being good at cricket? I could get used to that. It wasn't supporting Prince Naz even though he was Yemeni; it wasn't loving Bollywood movies like *Naseeb* or *Sholay* or *Maine Pyar Kiya* even though they were Indian; it was actual Pakistanis from Pakistan on the verge of being the best in the world.

It was the World Cup in which captain Imran Khan made his famous 'fight like cornered tigers' speech, because 'nothing is more dangerous than a cornered tiger'. The use of siege mentality as a psychological spur in sport is as old as sport itself – and certainly something Fergie knew a thing or two about – but it really spoke to the Pakistani against-all-odds attitude. I think there's a sense that most accomplishments both as individuals and as a nation are achieved *in spite* of circumstances or facilities or government, not because of them. Call it mercurial or maverick or downright chaotic but the Pakistani identity fits with the tiger analogy because it almost requires a hardship before a spectacular turnaround. That's how Imran framed the World Cup after a poor start which included losing to West Indies, India and South Africa in the round-robin stage of the tournament, and being incredibly lucky that rain saved them against, ironically, England. After his rousing big cat metaphor, Pakistan beat Australia in Australia, then Sri Lanka, and then New Zealand in New Zealand – twice.

Of course I didn't know any of this at the time. I was expecting to watch Graham Taylor's England draw 2–2 in Prague ahead of the Euros in Sweden. Instead I was introduced to a group of new heroes even more impressive than Paul Merson and Martin Keown. The only two players in the Pakistan side I was familiar with at the time were Imran Khan and Javed Miandad; Imran because he was probably the most famous Pakistani in the world and Javed almost by the osmosis of my mum watching (listening to) the cricket. As far as Imran is concerned, I put him in the same bracket as Bryan Robson and the Haçienda – legends that I was fixated with but probably around five years too young to witness at their peak. Still I saw enough to appreciate their massive influence on everything that followed. But I was at an age when I needed my own avatars of sporting prowess, not hand-me-downs.

That final, watched in a truncated format that only heightened the drama, brought the likes of Mushtaq Ahmed, Inzamam-ul-Haq and most importantly Wasim Akram into my life. There was one point late into the Pakistan innings when Inzy and Wasim were just slapping the ball to all ends of the ground and they took a moment to bump gloves and have a quick chat. My heart swelled with a national pride for Pakistan that I didn't know I had. Inzamam had only just turned 22, so was just a baby potato really, and he clearly hadn't developed a taste for ghee-heavy desi cooking yet. He was tall, broad and could still move quite spritely between wickets. Although he already had that almost benign aura of a big friendly giant – like a Pakistani Paul Bunyan with a bat instead of an axe. Wasim on the other hand was clearly a superhero. Just incredible with both bat and ball and capable of anything.

I love the story that Imran's sole direction to him was: 'Forget about no-balls. Just bowl fast.' A beautifully simple message that took away any fear of making mistakes and freed Wasim to express himself. There's a necessary recklessness about Pakistan at their best that just needs a tiny bit of harnessing to flourish. It's a trait that no one personified more than Shahid 'Boom Boom' Afridi, a maddening force of nature who could just as easily score a century from 37 balls as manage just 37 seconds on the pitch. But we're jumping ahead a genera-tion – I'm pretty sure Shahid still claims to be in his late twenties. Pakistan won the World Cup at the MCC and it ignited a sudden and overwhelming infatuation in me. I started obsessing over it like I obsessed over football.

Which brings me to a terrible confession. I, Nooruddean Choudry, am a recovering scrapbook addict. Anything to do with football, and for a time cricket, I'd turn into an A3 book of ripped out, clipped up and Pritt Stick'd memo-ries. And when I say 'addict' I'm only half-joking. It got to be a problem. At the beginning it started off small; taking clippings of note from the *Manchester Evening News* 'Pink' or the *Guardian*. I thought I could handle it. Then I began ripping up my magazine collection, as if I was a better curator of the content than the actual professional editors. Not only was I cutting and pasting the odd United- or Pakistan-related article, but I was going as big as taking out whole pages (that I could have just kept as intended in pristine magazine form) and as small as tiny 1 cm by 1 cm images in the adverts for new kits. I knew I had a serious problem when – and I believe me I'm not proud of this at all – it got so out of hand that I was taking books about United and Pakistan out of the library and … sorry … I was cutting pages and images out of those borrowed books for my scrapbook. I know, I know. I was abusing the trust of those very same institutions that had taught me so much about everything from football to world history, from *The Goon Show* to *Asterix & Obelix*. Fellow library members would be taking those very same books out after me sans the pages and images I'd stolen from the public purse. Oh the shame now. Back then I was an unthinking junkie desperate for my next fix. I've still got some of the scrapbooks. They're an odd, chaotic collection of the most random bits and bobs. Some would call them an archive; for me they're more a strange and slightly troubling insight into a scissor-happy little geek.

One thing 'the archive' does help with is telling a story of Pakistan's tour of England a few months after the

than in colourful one-day attire. Apart from everything else, I thought they were ever so handsome as a pair: tall, athletic, good-looking – Wasim reminded me a bit of the dad from *Blossom*, whereas I swear Waqar was Han Solo's Pakistani doppelgänger (except he'd break your toe with a yorker instead of shooting first). As individual talents they were clearly world-class but together they were something else entirely. A phenomenon; a happening. England's (very strong) batting line-up didn't stand a chance. My scrapbook very much agreed – but looked at things from a very different angle.

The yellowing clippings show that media coverage around the start of the series heavily referenced the infamous finger-wagging row between Mike Gatting and umpire Shakoor Rana during England's tour of Pakistan in the winter of 1987 – the last time they'd played each other in a Test series. There's a nice symmetry to that because the '92 Test ended with a nasty finger-pointing controversy of its own. The newspaper articles start off pretty convivial, and positively magnanimous in praise of Pakistan's bowling talents, but then you start to notice an ominous turn in the air. Fuelled by disgruntled murmurings coming out of the England camp, there's more and more pointed questions about how exactly Wasim and Waqar are able to get such wicked reverse-swing with the old ball, as if it can't possibly be down to talent. Those questions never quite turn into blatant accusations – at least not in the clippings I've got – but it's sort of worse because they just leave it hanging in the air like an eggy fart, contaminating something glorious.

There's one excerpt I have – from the *Daily Star* of all places – where England team manager Micky Stewart comes out with the particularly bitchy comment: 'I know how they do it, but I won't comment on whether it's fair or unfair.' Like I said – eggy. To me it just felt like another example of how they couldn't let us have *one* thing. Just one unambiguous, unsullied success. As with Prince Naseem, it had to be 'scandalous' and ill-gotten in some way. At least England captain Graham Gooch had the good grace and basic decency to offer unequivocal praise, admitting 'Pakistan were too good for us' and 'Pakistan rate with the very best; I've never come across two swing bowlers like Wasim Akram and Waqar Younis – it's their pace that makes them so devastating.' Michael Henderson of the *Guardian* summed it up when he said: 'Stewart appeared to suggest that he knew how Wasim and Waqar swung the old ball so prodigiously but he was not prepared to enlighten anyone including, one must assume, the England bowlers … surely it is enough to admit, as Graham Gooch did, that England were undone by two bowlers of exceptional ability.' Exactly. Thank you, Michael. Fuck that noise, and indeed, fuck Norman Tebbit. Pakistan Zindabad.

11.

NOT LEARNING BUT DROWNING

I am sure that the majority of boys currently attending Bury Grammar School quite enjoy being there. Or at least enjoy it as much as any kid 'enjoys' going to school. I'd also guess that most of the lads who went there at the same time as me share a similar approval rating for the old alma mater (see, Latin!). There wasn't anything especially terrible about the place then and I'd be very surprised if there is now. That said, I didn't enjoy my time there. It just wasn't for me in a number of fundamental ways.

Do you know that feeling when you walk into a meeting or formal event or a social gathering of some sort and within a few short moments of being there your heart sinks because you know you've got nothing in common with anyone else present and there's absolutely no point in you being there? When you desperately wish with every fibre of your being that you could turn right around and walk out, but you can't, so you just have to wait for merciful release? Well, that's pretty much how I felt for the entire seven years of my school life including sixth form. I'm trying not to make it sound dramatic because it wasn't really, and I am acutely aware that a lot of kids had and have it far worse than I did. I wasn't really bullied by anyone, I certainly wasn't abused in any way, and there wasn't some awful collective trauma that befell us of the kind that is all too common in the United States.

If I had a massive eraser that I could use to rub out a particular person or part of my school life to make everything better, I wouldn't know where to point the end of my pencil. I guess I'd just rub out every correct answer on my eleven-plus and not go there at all. My biggest issue with Bury Grammar is that I lost myself there. I was a happy, confident, overachieving kid and then I kind of just disappeared in that place – not to return properly until I left for uni. Don't get me wrong, outside of school with my family and my mates I was still me, but your time at school is so formative and character-building that of course it has an effect on you. They say that going to a good school and making the right sort of contacts can open up doors to you, and I suppose that's true if you make the most of it. But within yourself, if it douses that natural confidence and inner spark that makes you feel as if anything is possible, there's always the danger that you close off your own doors. You can go from fearless to doubting whether you'll ever do anything worthwhile.

At primary school I was always naturally good at stuff, and importantly, always felt that way. Anything new we'd learn or activity we'd try, I'd enter with gusto in the knowledge that I'd catch on quick and perform better than most. For instance, as previously mentioned I was always good at art (Terence can attest to that), and I'd always get praise from the teachers for my efforts. So much so that, one day, a teacher whose name I'll keep anonymous came in with a piece of wood and what looked like a kind of soldering iron (it might have just actually been one from B&Q). They asked me if I fancied having a go at creating a design on the piece of wood for their home – like a house name to put on the door. I can't remember what the name was – I'd never heard of a house having a name rather than just a number – but my instant reply was yes of course. I didn't give it a second thought. I'd never soldered anything in my life and my only woodwork experience was sharpening a pencil, but I had no doubt that I could do it and it'd be great. Looking back, the teacher in question should have had some doubts, leaving a kid alone with a piece of equipment that could very easily burn a hole through their hand or potentially even cause a fire, but those were simpler times. There probably wasn't a safety warning for kids not to solder pieces of wood just because an adult told them to. The point is, a confidence that verged on stupidity flowed through me. I was good at stuff. I could do it.

That's what I mean about the inner spark we've all got as kids, until something or someone puts it out. At Cravenwood, I was someone. Not only did I excel in any form of learning, but I was creative and funny with it too. I had quite a mature sense of humour that would come out in my work. For example, there was one time when we were tasked with writing a story, and mine ended with an overly dramatic cliffhanger suddenly interrupted by waking up in bed because 'it had all been a dream' (that go-to Dallas-style ending for any kid struggling for a fitting finale). But then that relief of being out of danger was suddenly interrupted *again* by waking up in the same perilous situation as before, because it was the waking up safe in bed bit that had been a dream. Talk about meta. The teachers loved me because I made them laugh and was never any bother. At that primary school age I had an unwavering self-belief, and just as important, people who believed in me. So much so that on one occasion a teacher was slightly perplexed at my mum's seeming indifference at her gushing over something I'd done, as if my mum wasn't that arsed about her son's achievement. It wasn't that – my mum was probably thinking, of course I'm proud but they always say nice things. She also had four other kids to sort out and pick up from school, so was a bit preoccupied with that too.

My demeanour at Cravenwood and then Bury Grammar was like chalk and cheese. There was obviously the afore-mentioned culture clash and feeling that I didn't belong on a class level that I've touched on already, but it was more than just that. As much as it all felt very posh and entitled and privileged to me, I don't want to give the wrong impression of the school as a whole or anyone who went there. It wasn't a boarding school or one of these properly rarefied public schools that actual toffs go to. It wasn't even an especially up-its-own-arse grammar school. There are different kinds of grammar school and I think Bury Grammar was/is a relatively normal one with a relatively normal intake of nice middle-class kids from nice middle-class families. The fact that I was from a far less privileged and moneyed background is what made it so foreign and 'posh' to me. In that respect it was more my problem and hang-up than a reflection of their hoity-toity culture. I never felt knowingly working-class or (relatively) poor before going to high school, because I was constantly around people who were in the exact same boat as me; Bury Grammar just happened to be a different, much fancier boat. A far bigger issue for me, more so than any difference in class or socio-economic standing, is that I went from a someone to a no-one.

Of course there is an overlap. Kids from affluent middle-class backgrounds generally tend to be a lot more self-assured and confident in themselves than those from disadvantaged circumstances; they've not grown up around the same stress and panic of parents having to face tough decisions about making ends meet and what basic essentials to do without. There aren't the same wrought tensions and secondary anxieties within a household so comfortable with covering utility bills and everyday expenses that there's disposable income to spare for 'quality time'. That's not to say that middle-class kids of means can't have a myriad of other issues that adversely affect their lives and complicate their childhoods, but they don't have that extra layer of trauma that comes from just trying to survive in fear of debt, malnutrition and bailiffs. At Bury Grammar, confidence and high achievement were rewarded; if you stood out in any way, you were given special treatment and individual focus. I don't mean being pulled out of class or selected for extra-curricular development, although that was part of it. I mean in lessons too. And to an extent there's nothing wrong with that. There's a meritocratic virtue in rewarding success. It's just the flipside of that was a neglect for anyone who was struggling. Or even worse, a complete indifference. It's really hard as a kid to go from feeling valued and capable of anything to completely unworthy of attention.

Having said all that, Sajid was the control. He was from a similar background to me with a lot of the same experiences. Granted he lived in a nice semi-detached house rather than a flat above a shop, went to Crumpsall Lane Primary (generally accepted as a bit more well-to-do than Cravenwood) and his family were probably a rung above us financially, but we had far more in common than most of the lads we went to school with. We were both from Cheetham Hill (his house was on the way to my library), both Muslim, both second-generation desi (albeit that his family was Indian Gujarati rather than Pakistani Punjabi) and both grew up working-class. Just as I'd help out in my father's shop, Sajid would wake up early to aid his dad at the markets. The difference being that Sajid was paid in pocket money and I was paid in 'experience'. With so much in common, with all else being equal, you'd expect us to have pretty similar experiences of assimilating to grammar school life. But that wasn't the case at all.

Whereas I floundered badly and disappeared into the background, Sajid positively flourished. He was a lot more streetwise and cocksure than me, which helped. I was different and it knocked me off course; Sajid was different and he wore it as a badge of honour. I envied the lack of fucks he gave. You know when you hear stories of a couple of promising starlets joining a top-flight club together from another country, and one of them takes to it with relative ease, posing happily with fish and chips, scoring a worldie in training and getting subbed on in a cup game within weeks of being there – while his pal struggles to adapt, rinses the Lebara phone card and desperately pines for home. It was a bit like that. I was very much the Jesús Navas to Sajid's David Silva, except I couldn't leave. Another important factor is that Sajid happened to be that most maddeningly annoying phenomenon – a casual genius. Even if I was good at a particular subject, I always struggled with exams. No matter how hard I crammed, nothing stuck. And I had a weird sort of stage fright, where I'd mess up the exam and immediately afterwards know what I should have done. Sajid was the complete opposite. He'd treat the whole revision process with open disdain, doss about for weeks, not stress in the slightest and absolutely ace everything. He was Will from *Good Will Hunting* – except in every single subject. Again, that's all that mattered at Bury Grammar. He didn't need help and so was part of the club. They only ever discriminated against thickos like me.

Still, I was so grateful Sajid was there. He was my best mate throughout my time at BGS and the one vital link between school and home. We could empathise with each other and have a good old bitch about everything, which I think are the two foundation stones of any great friendship. He saw the bright, funny, opinionated kid beyond the shit results and mute-buttoned shyness, and knew that he could speak candidly to me about stuff he wouldn't admit to others for fear of denting his cocky exterior. I think at school we must have seemed an odd combination – in-your-face Sajid and what's-his-face Noz – but I've always had mates like that; people who seem like an odd fit for me because they're far brasher or cockier and more trouble than little old me. The truth is always that they're genuinely lovely people underneath all that and I'm the real prick. A prick in non-prick's clothing. Schoolmates would occasionally see us dicking about at the bus stop or acting like idiots outside school and look slightly bemused at my out-of-character behaviour when that was the real me. There were a few others who knew what I was actually like, and, as ever, a lot of that was to do with football.

I don't think the power of football as a social lubricant can be overestimated. It instantly gives you something in common and a common shorthand. There's a reason why the very Partridge-esque trope of a middle manager type desperately trying to relate to a tradesperson in their home by way of tepid football chat rings so true – it's because it's exactly what happens all the time. Whether it's a pencil case with MUFC Tipp-Ex'd onto it that breaks the ice before double Chemistry or some shameless office brown-noser trying to suck up to their boss at the water-cooler, football as a subject is somehow common enough and personal enough to create a bond. Even if you're a misplaced little scrote at the wrong school.

Sajid was into football too, and a United fan to boot, but he wasn't really into it as much as me – or quite as obsessed at least. He knew enough to start an argument with a City or Liverpool fan, but not always enough to know how to win it. It was the only subject in which I was the A+ student and not him. The lads I ended up befriending most closely around football were Richard Blyth (Bolton Wanderers), Ben Mackenzie (United) and Elliott Levy (City). Really sound lads. Elliott was by far the most knowledgeable and a hardened season ticket holder at Maine Road (back when it was character building to say the least). Any time we'd have an argument that got out of hand he'd just say, 'Yeah and how many games have you been to?' The answer was still not many.

But even more bonding than talking about football was actually playing it. As previously mentioned, Sajid and I started off playing our weird 'can ball' invention, but we eventually realised how bizarre that was and graduated to an actual casey. As everyone knows, a football in a school yard is a magical thing. For the exact duration of a dinner hour or break time, it dissolves cliques, makes teammates out of relative strangers and does away with any social inhibitions. The golden rule is you're all equal, as long as the sides are equal. I made friends at school with kids who I didn't speak to properly despite weeks of playing football together. The kickabouts came first and then (eventually) the conversation. Instead we'd just communicate through one-two's, clattering tackles and the sporadic shouts of 'MAN ON!' and 'MINE!' and for a period after USA 94, yells of 'HAGGGIIIII!!!!' followed by stupidly unrealistic shots at goal.

Various players would come and go, but eventually we settled upon a number of regular mainstays who'd play every game. There was Sajid (obviously) – he was rapid and loved quick give-and-goes; we played with each other so often both in and out of school that we were practically telepathic – like an Asian Yorke and Cole – and deadly at Wembley doubles. I could go past players for fun with mazy dribbles (honestly!) but didn't have much pace. Fortunately concrete was perfect for me – it was slower than grass and definitely slower than skiddy astro, so the ball didn't get away. Then there was Anil Bhalla (good finisher, great shot especially on the volley); David Salad (our very own Darren Anderson, loved pegging it down the wing and getting a cross in); Paul Sherratt (good defender but sometimes played while eating an eggy sandwich); Michael Wheater (nice lad but a bit of a liability because he'd stomp about so enthusiastically that he'd inadvertently injure people with his big patent leather boots); Sachin Sinha (chaotic dribbler, head-down-and-run merchant); Andrew Whelan (really good player, technically maybe our best); and Simon Bunting (amazing engine and a great foil for Andrew). There were others but that was our main gang. We played at every possible opportunity. Even a few minutes before school was enough for a cheeky kickabout. If there wasn't enough of us or enough time for a proper game, we'd play Wembley singles or doubles, or 60 seconds (headers and volleys with a time limit).

I'm sure to look at we were a right old rabble of misfits, but playing football with those lads was honestly like a life raft for me. Out on that playground, I existed. It was a reason to look forward to going to school, rather than dread it with all my heart. I could endure being the invisible boy in lessons as long as I could come alive with the ball at my feet. It sounds corny, I know, but football was like a type of salvation from pointless anonymity. I look back at my school reports from those days and there's so much polite resignation about how much I'm struggling. It's as if they've already dismissed me as a lost cause. The general consensus is that I'm a well-behaved kid, very quiet, struggling with the work but that's okay because I'm doing my best. But it wasn't okay. Of course I didn't want angry reports saying I was a disgrace to the reputation of the school or anything like that, but it would have been infinitely better than essentially saying 'Yeah your boy's a bit rubbish innit ¯_(ツ)_/¯ At least a bit of negative feeling would have meant they hadn't yet given up on me doing any better. There's also more than a little hint of 'I don't really know this child very well or notice him very much so I'll just put something generic' in some of the reports, which is damning in its own way.

But amid all the resigned indifference there were a couple of teachers who did know who I was and could see a little something in me. Mr Burns, for example. He was Head of Art but built like a massive shithouse of a rugby player. I reckon he was definitely the cock of the staffroom. I don't think I ever saw him smile through his thick black beard; instead he had the kind of gruff no-nonsense aura that informed you never to even try to take the piss. He wasn't one to put his arm around me or give me the kind of inspiring pep talk you get in the movies, but in his own way he took an interest in what I was doing and encouraged me to express myself. I think he could tell that my brain worked a little differently from the other kids and that I'd always have a unique take on any class assignment. He was also hard on me, which I really appreciated. I'd be dead proud of something, and he'd tell me it's good but not great and how I could do so much better. That meant the world to me. It meant that he could see more in me than I could see in myself. Granted he may have expressed that sentiment in the style of a bulldog chewing on a wasp, but I liked that too. Usmaa – who went to the girls' school for a couple of years for her A-Levels – got talking to him once and apparently he raved about how talented I was. I was buzzing when I heard that.

Art was the one thing that got me any attention, in so much as it allowed me to express myself and show my true personality. We had a teacher called Mr Brotherton who taught me Business Studies (and I think for a brief period Maths). He was arguably the most popular teacher in the school because he was funny, charismatic and actually treated the kids with a level of mutual respect. Although he was certainly no pushover, he allowed a bit of banter in class. He was also a massive Leeds United fan so we could chat football with him, or rather others would. I kept my head down. Except there was one lesson in which I was surreptitiously reading the *Red Issue* fanzine under my desk. I was obsessed with *Red Issue* – its content was so age-inappropriate and disgusting and vulgar and I loved it. It was like *Viz*, which I also loved, except even rummer. They were just as merciless about United as they were about rival clubs, and full of mucky innuendo which was of course hugely appealing to me at that age (funnily enough, many years later I became a regular contributor to the print version of *RI* doing artwork).

One day I was so consumed with my contraband reading material that I didn't notice Mr Brotherton shuffle up beside me. He asked me what I was reading and of course I was absolutely mortified. I said sorry and handed over the fanzine and he told me to pay attention in class. I sat there with my cheeks burning with embarrassment until I looked up to see him casually leafing through my confiscated copy of *RI* at his desk with a grin on his face. After the lesson he handed it back and we got talking about football. He loved – and was clearly a bit surprised – that I was a (Manchester) United fan and took to ribbing me about it at every opportunity. I became his designated Red to mock and rib whenever we lost or Leeds won. I loved that. It gave me some kind of identity. One Business Studies lesson we were tasked to come up with examples of effective marketing to a particular demographic. I decided to take a bit of inspiration from *Red Issue* and presented my homework in the form of a little comic strip showing United fans arriving in Galatasaray to a banner saying 'Welcome to the Hell', as was the case in 1993. Under the banner I'd put the various selling points of hell as a holiday destination. Mr Brotherton loved it and kept my exercise book to show the other teachers.

A few days later, Mr Benger, who taught Music and Drama at the school but didn't actually teach me anything, popped his head around our form classroom door and asked if he could 'borrow me'. Wondering whether I was in trouble for something, I followed him into the corridor. He explained he'd seen my Galatasaray cartoon via Mr Brotherton, and wondered whether I'd like to contribute to the school's annual magazine, *The Clavian*. He essentially told me that I had carte blanche to take the piss out of any of the teachers over a couple of pages because I was 'clearly a very funny chap'. I couldn't believe it. I said yes of course I'd do that.

The Clavian was a mostly dry, rather austere publication that served as an official record of the school year and various outstanding achievements of the pupils. Suffice to say there was no other way I'd be in it. It dated all the way back to the 1880s and included stuff like an editorial from the Headmaster; obituaries for Old Boys (that's what they called former pupils – I'm not just being overly familiar about dead OAPs); summaries of field trips to places like Riga and Cologne; an annual report on the school's Combined Cadet Force (they'd have camo'd up lads walking around the school wearing full army fatigues – very weird); and a list of winners of awards called things like 'The Oliver Entwistle Memorial Prize for the Captain of the School' and 'The Cecil John Turrell Cronshaw Prizes for Chemistry' (both real). And in between all that Mr Benger wanted my daft wee cartoons.

Looking back, I took my editorial freedom *way* too far. Especially where I've drawn Mr Hone literally as Adolf

Hitler, complete with the side-parting, trademark moustache and whip(!?), 'Keep those pens moving, comrades!' (I think I got my evil despots mixed up there.) Another needlessly cruel one features Mrs Glancy, who was known for her excessive use of perfume; I have her starring in *Scent of a Woman*, overpowering Al Pacino with her stink. The worst one, and I'm not proud of this, is of PE teacher Mr Koziura – who walked with a very noticeable limp. I've called him Mr 'funny walk' Koziura, dressed him as a pirate with a peg leg (just to drive the point home), and there's a speech bubble saying: 'I'm similar to the Oldham Athletic manager – we've both got bad sides!' Terrible, I know. Firstly, what the hell was I thinking? Secondly, what the double hell was Mr Benger thinking?! Censor me, for fuck's sake! The cartoons went down a storm (because kids are inherently cruel) and there was a general sense of shock that I was capable of such dark humour.

Most of the other cartoons are football-related and very much of their time. I have Liverpool fan Mr Sherlock on the touchline at Anfield, ordering Ian Rush to take a dive in the box; Mr Brotherton (of course) bemoaning United's title win and listing a load of mitigating factors; Mr Hateley teaching Eric Cantona French (any sense of logic went out of la fenêtre with that one); and City fan Mr Armsbey wearing an Umbro kit that says 'Why bother?' instead of 'Brother' with the mocking headline 'Another great new dawn at Maine Road' (how times change). Amazingly, all the teachers took it in their stride (no pun intended, Mr Koziura) and I even had one or two stop in the corridor saying stuff like, 'You better not do me next year, Choudry!', which roughly translated to *please* do me next year. It gave me a nice kind of notoriety I'd not experienced before and lasted a week or so, before I went back to being largely unknown.

The only other thing that made me stand out was less pleasant and frankly a bit odd. In a trait that a lot – but not all – of Asian people share for some reason, I wasn't a very good swimmer. In fact I was pretty rubbish. I'm not sure why that was the case considering I'd regularly visit the extremely Victorian (i.e. beautiful and crumbling) Harpurhey swimming baths when I was at Cravenwood. Maybe it was because I faffed about in the shallow end too much, aided with floats and armbands. Anyway, my lack of proficiency in the water was very evident to the rest of our class as well as the PE teacher. I'd kick around a lot but get nowhere fast and eventually end up flailing for the side of the pool. The thing with Mr PE was he had a reputation for being a little sadistic – or at the very least he had a very twisted sense of humour. Any boy who forgot their kit was threatened with the punishment of wearing a girl's swimming costume instead (although I never saw that actually happen). His solution to my chlorine-stinking troubles was to hand me a pair of comically oversized black flippers, as if I was a deep-sea diver. There were other kids who were similarly weak at swimming but they weren't lumbered with flippers – just me. So every swimming lesson I'd come out of the changing room and have to moonwalk the entire length of the pool – the other option being to walk forwards lifting my knees to their highest point before slapping them down on the wet floor with every step. All the other boys would find the sight (and sound) of me hilarious, while Mr PE would stand there with a stupid little smirk on his face. I wish I could say it was character-building but it really wasn't. Just needlessly humiliating. Suffice to say, I had the last laugh – I still can't swim.

Unfortunately no amount of cartoons or swimming aids could improve my academic performance. I don't think I was a thick child by any means, but results and general performance in lessons don't exactly help my argument. On a very basic level, Bury Grammar knocked all the confidence out of me. It made me doubt whether I was smart, which has the same effect as being dumb. Even when I knew the answer to a question proffered in class, self-doubt and shyness (along with a stutter that got worse when I was nervous) did for me and I just kept schtum. English was the worst for that. We'd be covering a set text like *Macbeth* or *Doctor Faustus* and we've be asked to interpret what a particular scene or soliloquy might signify; in my head I was coming up with loads of great answers but then never uttered a word. Instead I'd listen to some shit response like 'it means blood is really hard to wash off' and silently curse them for getting Shakespeare wrong.

It can't be overstated enough how vital confidence is to the development of a child. I honestly think that's one of the biggest things that stops working-class kids from fulfilling their potential – their middle-class counterparts aren't any brighter, they just carry themselves with more self-assurance and communicate more effectively. Again, it's a by-product of feeling you belong. They should teach (or rather coach) public speaking at a young age to level the playing field just a little. I was petrified of anything like that, so just melted into the background, and most of the teachers seemed happy enough for me to stay there. I think Bury Grammar was heavily geared towards getting the most out of high-achieving kids.

If you were thriving academically, you'd be given extra attention to get even better. Even if you were smart, the onus was on making you smarter, which is great. But below that, for anyone struggling like me, I think it was just accepted that, unfortunately, you were going to fall by the wayside. You were collateral damage in the real aim to get as many high-flying kids into Oxbridge as possible. If you were more likely to get into Salford than Oxford then you were very much an afterthought – if that. I don't want to sound too negative about Bury Grammar because a lot of kids clearly thrived there. Maybe the problem was me. But I often wish that I'd gone to another school. Just a normal school like my mates. Perhaps I would have continued to fly with confidence; and even if I did struggle, at least be put into a lower set with the chance to do well in there. It was just a bad signing. I was like Karel Poborsky at United. No one's fault as such, but wrong place at the wrong time.

In a tragicomic denouement to my time at Bury Grammar, Sajid and I made our way to Bury on the 135 bus to collect our A-Level results. I knew I'd done shit, but the weeks in between the exams and results can play funny tricks on your brain. You forget the blind panic you felt at leafing through the questions and not having a clue where to start, and the heart-sinking feeling of hearing 'Okay, pens down' when you were nowhere near done. You start to fool yourself into thinking you didn't actually do that badly – especially if your best mate is (justifiably) brimming with confidence. Walking into school was kind of strange. Everyone was wearing normal clothes and it suddenly dawned on us all that this was the last time we'd set foot in the place. I was hit by a strange mix of emotions. Seven years I'd spent at Bury Grammar and hated most of it. Now I felt a sense of loss. I wasn't going to miss it, but there was a queasy hollowness inside me, thinking about what a waste of potential it had all been. I'd never be at school again and suddenly I was desperate to redo it from the start and maybe do it right this time. But that was that. All that was left was to find out if I'd salvaged anything at all with my A-Level results. Sajid and I picked up our envelopes and decided we'd open them at Bury Interchange. We'd arrived there together by train on our first day at school; now we'd be leaving together on the new Metrolink tram.

Arriving at the interchange we sat down to reveal our individual fates. Sajid opened his envelope and smiled broadly. I opened mine and did not. It was worse than I'd feared. Sajid, bless him, tempered his own joy by giving me some words of encouragement. I appreciated it but wasn't really listening. After a moment to compose myself, I schlepped over to the pay phone to ring home. My dad answered and I relayed my results one by one. There was silence at the other end of the line. A long ominous silence. It went on for so long I was going to ask if he was still there. Eventually, my dad responded with 'Inna Lillahi wa inna ilayhi raji'un.' It's a verse from the Qur'an which means 'Verily we belong to Allah and verily to him do we return.' It's what you say when someone dies. I put the receiver back on the hook and told Sajid. All he could offer at that stage was 'Oh, mate.' It was so utterly devastating and heartbreaking that I burst out laughing, and so did Sajid. We wouldn't stop. I wondered whether I could sneak into Salford through clearing.

12.

NO SUCH THING AS FERGIE TIME

You never know where life will take you. We all have a start point and an end point, and the line between the two can be so muddled. It always freaks me out when people occasionally share these daft little websites that supposedly tell you when you're going to die. It's nonsense of course; just a randomly generated date in the future based on nothing but how that particular algorithm is coded. But I still don't like them. To see a date, no matter how arbitrary, makes me feel funny inside. No one needs to know, or even speculate, about where or when their journey will end. It's best to crack on and leave that to God, or fate, or whatever you believe in. That said, it doesn't make it any less fascinating to examine the lives of those who have already left us. That's a different story; a completed story. Even if you didn't know them.

I've always had a morbid interest in cemeteries, maybe because I spent my childhood living opposite one. Just walking past headstones, reading the messages of love and loss and the side-by-side dates of beginnings and ends, is both fascinating and sobering. Each tells a story about who that person was, what they were like and who they left behind. Sometimes the two dates are tragically close together, others span centuries, world wars and revolutions. What they all have in common is someone cared enough to remember them. I always find it really upsetting when I hear about bodies being moved from their burial sites, or even whole cemeteries being excavated for the sake of commercial property development. Wesleyan Methodist Cemetery, next to where we lived, no longer exists. Nor does my dad's shop, or the precinct it was part of, or indeed our old flat. It was all demolished and dug up for the sake of a giant Tesco's. I'm rubbish with bearings, but I'm pretty sure the box room I shared with my brother is now the frozen peas aisle.

It's sad that it's all gone, but that's the way of the world. For me, what's far worse than bulldozing our old gaff (without so much as a commemorative blue plaque) is that the cemetery was desecrated. People buried their loved ones there, leaving tender epitaphs on slabs of stone they thought would stand forever. Now it's a car park. In 2003, over 20,000 bodies were exhumed from that site and dumped into mass graves in Bury and Blackley. Distraught relatives were told it would cost around £3,000 for individual reburials but then were not given time to raise the money. Rampant consumerism waits for no one, dead or alive.

Sir Matt Busby is buried in the Roman Catholic section of Southern Cemetery, on Barlow Moor Road, alongside his wife Jean. Their shared headstone has no reference to Manchester United or even football, and instead describes them as a 'beloved wife' and 'devoted husband', a 'much-loved mother' and 'loving father', and a 'dear nanna and grandad'. As it should be. There's always the odd piece of Manchester United memorabilia laid down by a fan along-side fresh flowers: a scarf or a MUFC teddy. But it's a dignified and modest resting place for a dignified and modest man. Southern Cemetery is one of the largest cemeteries in the country, and so Sir Matt is not without esteemed company. Manchester's first multi-millionaire and philanthropist John Rylands – in whose name the city's most beautiful library was built – is also buried there (albeit with a much grander memorial), as are the artist LS Lowry, Maria Pawlikowska-Jasnorzewska, the Polish poet, Factory Records founder Tony Wilson (with a head-stone designed by Peter Saville) – and fellow Factory icons Rob Gretton and Martin Hannett. They all came from different places and lived vastly different lives, and yet they ended up in the same place.

I think of Sir Matt as a young kid in the small Lanarkshire village of Orbiston, having no idea what destiny awaited him and how important a rainy post-industrial city in England would be in defining his future. I know all about Busby's upbringing because I'd constantly read up about it and watch programmes about his life. My favourite was a three-part Arena documentary called *The Football Men* by my favourite journalist, Hugh McIlvanney (I used to ask my dad if we could get the *Sunday Times* just so I could read his articles). *The Football Men* was about the lives and careers of Busby, Jock Stein and Bill Shankly, who were all born within a 20-mile radius of each other and all became the greatest managers at their respective clubs. Obviously I was most interested in Busby's story, but I loved the idea that there was something unique about where these three legends were born and bred that somehow made them so special. McIlvanney's documentary series was as captivating and beautifully crafted as his prose. His voice was so warm and hypnotic that he could have said that all three managers landed in Bellshill from the planet Mars and I'd have believed it. I recorded *The Football Men* on a VHS tape from my dad's shop, as I did with anything remotely to do with United, and watched it all the time. When Busby died at the age of 84, not long after my fifteenth birthday, of course I watched it again.

Maybe I overdid it. As well as all my various Busby-related tapes, including the official history of Manchester United and a documentary about the Munich air disaster, there was wall-to-wall coverage of his passing on both national and regional news. Granada TV did some great segments about his life and achievements, as did *North West Tonight* and *Grandstand* too. There's always a tendency to binge on a famous person's legacy when they die. It's the same way people watch a classic film when one of the cast passes away or stream the back catalogue of a favourite pop star when they expire. For some it's a type of mourning, but I think for most people it's more the fact we're suddenly reminded about how great they were in all the tributes and obituaries, and so we feel compelled to savour it all over again. When you combine that instinct with a nerdy teenager's obsession with football, it's a heady mix.

I was bingeing on so much Busby-related coverage in the immediate aftermath of his death that it pissed my dad off. And not just because I was monopolising the telly. In a fit of temper he shouted at me to 'turn that bloody thing off' and that he was 'sick of that man's face'. I was taken aback. What was his problem with Matt Busby's face? And why was he angry with me? Then with the same anger, but slower, almost like he was emphasising each word to make me understand, he said: 'He is not your dad.' I was speechless. What the hell did he mean? I went from feeling concerned about being told off to quite angry at him back. What kind of thing was that to say? Of course I knew Matt Busby wasn't my bloody dad. You're my dad. I didn't even want Matt fucking Busby to be my dad. I switched off the TV and marched out of the room without saying a word. I could feel that my ears were burning red and could feel I was going to cry so I went straight to the bathroom. I didn't know why he'd said that. 'He is not your dad.' I didn't know why he was so angry with me. I didn't even know why I was angry now. Angry to the verge of tears. I had a bit of a cry in the bathroom and then washed my face so no one would notice, but it was pointless because my nose was now redder than Fergie's post-hairdryer. I didn't go back to the living room and just went to my room to listen to the radio.

Looking back, I wish I had the emotional intelligence to deal with that moment differently. I think my dad had me completely wrong and was hurt by something that wasn't true. Of course it was a sad thing that Busby had passed away, but it's not like I was going through some intense grieving process. Sir Matt Busby was integral to the history of the club that I love. And his impact on United can't possibly be measured in terms of the trophies he won. Five league titles, two FA Cups and one European Cup don't even begin to tell the full story. All that is good about the club began with him. So of course, I found him a compelling figure and put him on a bit of a pedestal. My dad would encourage me to read about great people in history, especially leaders, and I didn't see how Busby didn't fit squarely into that category. Plus there was the fact that any public appearance of him in my lifetime was that of a lovely, smiling old man. But I didn't have any massive emotional attachment to him beyond an affectionate admiration and respect.

I wish I could have just told my dad exactly that, there and then. And also told him – as if it needed saying – that I loved him. Regardless of my feelings towards Busby, it breaks my heart to think that my dad was even a little bit resentful of how I might have felt about anyone else, or that he harboured the slightest doubt about my feelings towards him. It makes me feel like I failed as a son. That I didn't make my love for him obvious enough. The thing is, even if I could quantum leap back like Sam Beckett to redo that day, I'm not entirely sure how he would take it. Whether it would assuage his angry upset or make it even worse. I don't know if he'd take such naked acknowledgement of our relationship from me in the spirit and love it would be intended, or if it would rile him that I was laying it all out in such plain terms. Maybe I'd come across as a precocious little shit trying to dad my own dad. But I wish there was a way of telling him that he was being daft to even momentarily question my love for him.

Thinking about it, instead of quantum-leaping back to the mid-1990s, maybe a DeLorean would be better. That way I'd get to speak to my dad as a proper grown-up. Something I never got the chance to do. We'd be able to talk on the same level, without the father/son dynamic getting in the way. I don't think he got to know me properly and I certainly didn't get to know him. He was always such a dominating figure in that old-school Asian dad way, maintaining a hard line of authority that was impossible to break through back then. So much so that we didn't really have conversations as such. It would mainly be lectures; him talking and me listening, bar the odd one-word answer to mostly rhetorical questions.

I'd often think twice about asking him the most casual, inoffensive question because it would start off with him giving me a simple answer, and then slowly turn into a prolonged learning moment. I'd hope for a brief explanation but then find myself sat in the same spot, nodding away a couple of hours later, with a numb arse and feet prickly with pins and needles. More often than not it would eventually turn into a telling off for something it wasn't even about, like not having a hobby (a productive one, not football) or wasting too much time dossing about with my friends when I could have been learning a skill or working in the shop. I'm sure he didn't sit there waiting for me to ask a dumb question so he could trap me for the rest of the afternoon and make me feel bad about myself. I'm certain that he welcomed an opportunity for us to chat, but those 'chats' would unfortunately end up morphing into these existential monologues about how I was wasting my time. From his point of view I don't think he thought of his lectures as a punishment, just his way of providing some guiding words to make me a better person. But for any of the wisdom I did absorb (and you have to appreciate I was a teenager and therefore at my very least receptive to any parental guidance) the real cost of these prolonged tellings-off was never getting to properly know my dad and vice versa. And I really don't think that was a price worth paying.

We never got past that hardened respect-your-elders and speak-when-spoken-to stage. I look around the community I was brought up in and still live among – the Asian diaspora community – and there are so many cases of the strictest, most uncompromising and authoritarian of dads from that generation going all soft in their old age. They now laugh benignly at stuff they'd go mad over and pick mangoes instead of constant faults. Do you remember how everyone hated/feared Fergie back in the day because he was such a watch-tapping, official-berating, boot-kicking, cup-smashing, journalist-bollocking and winning-at-all-costs force of nature, and now he's sweet old adorable Fergie with his *Last of the Summer Wine* cap? It's like that with Asian dads now, except sitting in a mosque or a temple instead of Old Trafford. So complete does the transformation from dictator to sweetheart tend to be that the latest batch of apna kids – still only the third generation in this country – can't even fathom that their mischievous elderly accomplices could ever have laid down the law to anyone. If only they knew. I love it though, the mellowing of strict parents to more chilled-out versions of themselves. It means you can become more like their friends – albeit with a natural respect that never goes away.

There's a bit in *The Godfather* that always gets me. It's when Michael Corleone, now the de facto head of the family, is talking to his ailing father Vito in the garden. Vito is frail at this point and keeps flitting between thoughts and half-sentences while trying to advise his son. Michael tells him not to worry and assures him that everything is under control. After telling his son that he didn't want this life for him, there's a bit where Vito, acutely aware of his own mortality, says wistfully: 'There wasn't enough time, Michael. There just wasn't enough time.' That's kind of how I feel about my dad. I wish there had been more time to get to know each other. Maybe even just another five or ten years. It couldn't have happened while he was still alive, because he was still so entrenched in his role as hardened patriarch and I was practically a kid. But given a few extra years, we could have turned into something approaching friends. Not quite that, but near enough. The reason Vito wanted more time with Michael was to provide him with extra guidance and advice, whereas I got that all the time whether I wanted it or not. I needed that extra time to grow a bit closer to my dad; to experience that mellower version I see in others. I wanted to see him smile more and relax into old age.

They say you can judge a man by the company he keeps. And by that logic, my dad was far more open, relaxed, and progressive and a funnier guy than I knew him to be. To me he was still very much an authority figure who set the rules and expected you to follow them without question or debate. He was conservative with a small (and I suspect big) 'C'. But so many of his friends were the loveliest, most interesting people. As much as helping out at my dad's shop was a chore – made more bearable by the fact that he sold televisions so I could watch teletext and *Grandstand*, albeit with the sound off – I did love it when his friends would come in for a cup of tea and a chat. The 1990s were not a good decade for my dad's independent hi-fi store; Rumbelows had opened up around the corner on Cheetham Hill and their range and discounted prices were taking away a lot of custom. The very scant consolation for our dwindling family income was that there was more time for my dad's pals to come in for a good chinwag. They could drink cups upon cups of tea (made by muggins here) while nattering away, and rarely be disturbed by the inconvenience of a paying customer.

My dad clearly had a no dickhead rule for his inner circle of friends because they were all so sound. And such an eclectic bunch too. There was Martin, who worked for my dad doing repairs, and had a wonderfully sardonic sense of humour; Andrew, the palest Italian man with darkest jet black hair who was as daft as a brush and reminded me of Mickey Pearce from *Only Fools and Horses*; Les Rose, a dear old Jewish gentleman who was softly spoken, full of wisdom and ever so kind to me (and the only person my dad would listen to about being too strict in telling me off); Barclay Jackson, an athletic rugby-playing academic who was utterly charming and always spoke to me like I was one of the adults (which of course I loved); and Susan, a trans woman my dad had known since before her gender reassignment, who was very obviously going through difficult times with her mental health (judging from her chats with my dad) but always checked on everyone else to make sure they were okay. And then there was Muhammad Ali, who knew my dad from when they both worked together in a plastics factory in the 1960s. They became friends after he intervened when some white colleagues were giving my dad a hard time. Muhammad (which wasn't his name at the time) was an amateur boxer from his days back in Jamaica, and so they wisely did as they were told. Through his friendship with my dad, Muhammad developed a love for Islam which led to him converting (or 'reverting' as it is often termed) to the religion. He later opened his famous Peace and Love Barber Shop in Moss Side. He, like nearly all of my dad's friends, fascinated me endlessly. They were clearly all fond of my dad in a way that suggested there were so many facets of his personality I never knew.

Some of that was my fault. In retrospect, there were definitely times when my dad would allow the slightest crack to show in his hardened veneer and hint at opening up, and I just didn't respond. Like I said, I was at the worst age for that. For most of us I think there's a very obvious inverted bell curve for how much we admire and appreciate our parents. It starts off high because they're essentially your world and your first real heroes; then it drops down to a low during your adolescent years, when you realise they're not actually perfect and you resent their flaws; and then eventually it picks back up when you're old enough to appreciate their unconditional love and cherish them all the more *because* of their flaws – because they did everything they could for you in spite of not being perfect and having all the answers. It is safe to say that I was at my nadir of fully appreciating my dad. I remember watching TV once and New Order were on. It was that mad performance on *Top of the Pops* when they were playing 'Regret' on Malibu Beach with David Hasselhoff looking on. While I was watching, half loving and half hating the bonkers juxtaposition, my dad casually remarked, 'He used to come into the shop.' I just looked around, gave him the minimum acknowledgement and carried on watching the telly. As if anyone from New Order would ever have stepped foot inside my dad's shop! What a strange lie, I thought to myself.

Many years later I was reading the book *Substance* by the band's bassist Peter Hook. He talks about how Rob Gretton moved their rehearsal space from Pinky's in Broughton to an old gas board building 'next to a graveyard in Cheetham Hill, where they worked on songs for 'Power, Corruption & Lies'. He goes on to reference a little store in the 'shopping precinct next door' that he'd pop into occasionally for equipment. That wasn't the only cool thing to happen there. In the 1980s, my dad used to organise qawwali jamming sessions in the basement of his shop that he'd record on pretty state-of-the-art technology for that time. They featured none other than Nusrat Fateh

Ali Khan, who signed a CD for my brother and I, and Abida Parveen, who even came up to the flat for some tea. She had mad hair, a loud voice and complimented my mum on her palak gosht. We never talked about stuff like that, and I really wish we had. The only cultural reference points that my dad knew I shared with him were the music of Nat King Cole, the films of Jimmy Stewart and, right towards the end, the poetry of Muhammad Iqbal.

The summer of 1997 was one of change. Despite my rubbish A-level results, I just about managed to scrape into Salford University to study economics. I'd always harboured dreams of one day becoming a journalist and figured the best way to do that would be to have a specialism. Never in a million years was anyone ever going to pay me to write about football, so I thought why not economics? After all, I was the second-best performing pupil in the whole year for economics at A-level and stressed that to Salford when making my case to be let in. The bit I left out was the fact there were only two of us in the whole year actually doing economics. But still, facts are facts – even half ones. Part of what attracted me to going to Salford was that their degree promised the opportunity to spend a semester in Kamloops in British Columbia, Canada. I'd never been abroad on my own and it just seemed like a great way of doing it – in such a lovely setting too. The photos looked so beautiful, with mountains and lakes and wildlife parks. A far cry from Salford Precinct and Peel Park (as smashing as they were in their own way).

There were also winds of change blowing through Old Trafford. We had now officially entered the post-Cantona era. After four titles in five years (the odd-one-out being 1994/95 when he was suspended for 'kicking the hooligan'), Eric was leaving us at only 30 years of age. It seemed so needlessly premature, but that was Eric – departing just as suddenly and dramatically as he arrived. He was off to enjoy life, write poetry, play beach football and pursue a career in acting. We could hardly complain – he had given us enough memories and magic and gasps of disbelief in his five years with us to last a lifetime. It just meant there was a massive dock-off hole in our team and our hearts that needed filling. There were plenty of names rumoured to be replacing the irreplaceable, including Roberto Baggio from Juventus (if only!) and Juninho from Middlesborough (I'd have been more than happy with that). The absolute dream – maybe even more than Baggio who was slightly older – was Gabriel Omar Batistuta, who was not so much a centre-forward as a walking special effect. If he'd have signed it would almost have made up for Eric leaving. In the end, after much speculation, we replaced the most iconic and enigmatic player in the club's history with … Teddy Sheringham. It was underwhelming to say the least. I mean, he was a fine player no doubt, but he just seemed like such a huge downgrade from the King.

That summer there was even a bit of room to breathe in our crowded flat. My brother, Usmaa, Saadia and my dad were off to Mecca to perform Umrah (like a mini version of the Hajj pilgrimage that can be undertaken at any time) and then on to Pakistan. That left me, my mum and Ayesha at home. I was gutted not to be going for Umrah, but at the same time glad I could just chill at home instead of going to Pakistan. Don't get me wrong, it's not like I didn't want to revisit Sahiwal and Arifwala and see all my relatives again after seven years away; it's just that I was looking forward to hanging out with my mates for a few weeks and not having to worry about exams and stuff. And if I'm absolutely truthful, it was also that my dad would be away so there'd be a far more relaxed vibe at home. I just imagined going to Pakistan and second-guessing everything I did around my dad and him giving me lectures about not wasting time having fun all day when I could be preparing for university by reading up on Adam Smith and John Maynard Keynes. It sounds bad and it really was. I basically wanted to spend the summer apart from my dad rather than with him, which in hindsight is quite shitty and I regret thinking that way. But it's not like I turned down the opportunity to go. Last time it was me and Ayesha and so this time it was taken for granted it would be Usmaa, Saadia and Razi. They actually had a cracking time in Pakistan (after the uniquely beautiful experience of Umrah) and would rave about it over the phone. It sounded like dad was surprisingly chilled out with them and let them go off on adventures with the cousins while he spent as much quality time as possible with his parents and brothers and sisters after so long away.

Meanwhile, back in Manchester we were enjoying the extra space, albeit with plenty of jobs to do around the flat. It was more dilapidated than ever and so we were kept busy fixing things and patching things up. The precinct landowners were in no rush to make it any more hospitable, or indeed liveable. In fact they were banking on us pissing off. We later learnt that they'd been trying to get rid of us for some time and my dad had been trying his best to keep them at bay. There was also money owed. Me, my mum and Ayesha were literally trying to fix leaks in the ceiling with polyfilla and continually trying to scrub off/paint over mould on the walls. Even the silverfish were thinking of moving out. We also started to hear people breaking into the precinct at night and occasionally smashing windows. That was new. In a laughable effort to keep us safe, I took to sleeping with a cricket bat next to my bed. What was I going to do? Practise my reverse-sweep while they nicked the telly? I think the one thing keeping us safe is that no one would imagine anyone was actually living there.

The Pakistan party returned with hockey sticks, reams of colourful fabrics and a suitcase full of stories. It sounded like they'd had a blast and there were even a few in-jokes they were sharing with dad. I think from dad's point of view it had been something of a bittersweet experience. He'd enjoyed catching up with everyone and spending time there, but he made a few references to my mum about how things had changed. Some of that was the towns and villages he used to know so well, but I think some of it referred to family. He was not so much angry and annoyed about it, more resigned and a bit sad. I can't imagine what it's like to leave your home for a new life somewhere else and then find yourself as an inbetweener – not fully welcomed and accepted in your new surrounds but yet irreparably detached from the old. That place you left no longer exists. My dad, referring to Usmaa, Saadia and Razi (and all of us, I suppose) said we were so innocent and naïve compared to the kids over there – and I don't think he meant that as a criticism. I think he was right. I think we were pretty innocent and naïve for kids over here too.

The start of university was exciting, though, and would hopefully serve to grow me up a bit in that respect. It's not like I was moving away, but still the freedom they gave you to succeed or fail on your own terms – and their emphasis on getting the most out of the experience outside of just the academic side – was a breath of fresh air compared to Bury Grammar. Pretty early on I met a lad who would become one of my best mates – Aasim Aziz. He was as different from Sajid as it was possible to be. Relentlessly jolly and gregarious, he was like a cross between Salman Khan and Alan Partridge in the nicest possible way. Just a ray of sunshine. He was always perfectly turned out in designer clothes, but the type of designer clothes that someone in their thirties would wear.

Finally I had a friend who was more Carlton Banks than me. Finally I could be the Will Smith. We got talking about Kamloops and he was even more excited than me. I could already see him there, adjusting his side-parting in the bracing wind, a Ralph Lauren jumper from Kendals draped and knotted over his shoulders.

In the end, I didn't make it to British Columbia. But Aasim did, and he kept in touch through this new thing called electronic mail. You could send and receive photos on it that would appear on your screen in a matter of minutes via the internet superhighway, which was like teletext but interactive. But then I had slightly more pressing issues to deal with at home.

On 6 January 1998 – one day before my brother's birthday and three days before mine – my dad was rushed to North Manchester General. We found him awake but unable to respond in the living room. He'd had a stroke. That Tuesday was the last time we were a family of seven in that flat. We each took turns to be at his bedside, praying to Allah that he'd be okay. The doctor told us in a necessarily blunt but sensitive manner that he wasn't going to make it. Every day he got worse: from being able to look at us, to being able to squeeze a hand in his, to the slightest of movements of recognition when we spoke to him. In the end, all we could do is be with him, pray silently, stroke his head and occasionally wet his dry lips.

On 15 January 1998, Muhammad Siddique Choudry died of a brain haemorrhage caused by a stroke. I hope that this doesn't sound morbid or weird but being there by his side when he passed away is one of the proudest moments of my life. I *think* that's what I mean. I hope 'proud' is the right word. I just mean that I've never been more honoured to be anywhere than with my dad at that moment. I'd not been the perfect son to him – not by a long shot – but I was at least there for him in his last moments. We don't know where or when our journey will end but the most we can hope for is that we're not alone when the time comes. And my dad wasn't. That made me proud. *Inna Lillahi wa inna ilayhi raji'un.* Like Sir Matt Busby, he's buried in Southern Cemetery. He was 56 years old.

There's nothing like your dad dying to make you grow up fast. I was still a teenager barely into my first year of university, but as the oldest son I instantly became the 'man of the house'. I knew that because everyone kept reminding me. Every single visitor who came to pay their respects would tell me that I had to take responsibility now and look after my mum and my brothers and sisters. As if I didn't know. I remained respectful and nodded my head to each of them dutifully. They meant well, or at least most of them did. One thing I really resented was visitors who would purposely try to upset my mum. I don't know if this is just an Asian thing or an everyone thing, but the number of aunties who would come in, not say a word and hold my mum in an endless embrace until she broke down in tears. They wouldn't let go until she broke down, whispering things like 'It's okay, it's okay,' and 'Be brave, be brave,' knowing full well it would trigger her upset all over again. That sounds mean-spirited, as if I'm getting angry at something they didn't intend to do, but honestly it was intentional and emotionally draining for my mum. None of her close friends did that. They were more concerned with practicalities like bringing over food and asking if we needed any help.

I didn't cry in front of any visitors; I didn't even cry in front of the family. Only Sajid saw me crying, once, when we were chatting outside the flat and I couldn't hold back the tears. That's not me being stoic or brave or better than anyone who did cry openly, it was just how I coped with things. It's funny when you're in mourning for someone particularly close to you – both figuratively and sometimes even literally. You're so emotionally spent all the time, so much of a sponge for other people's sadness too, that occasionally you need a release. The five of us kids and even my mum would find ourselves laughing uncontrollably at the silliest of things. Like laughing until you get a stitch. I think it's a common thing. It's a necessary human instinct or coping mechanism or something. Otherwise you'd fall into a dark hole of misery and never come out. Eventually after the distraction of a good laugh or something on TV or even a mundane brainless task that needs doing, the enormity of your loss hits you again and you're sad. People can be genuinely caring and considerate and empathetic towards you and really mean it for that moment, but ultimately they go home and get on with their lives. It's only you and your direct family who have to live with it and deal with the consequences.

As much as the 'man of the house' moniker was passed on to me, I have to say that my two elder sisters – Ayesha and Usmaa – were incredible in just dealing with so much complicated admin and fallout from my dad's death. He'd always dealt with stuff like bills and rent and stuff like that himself – even though my mum would have been so much better at it than him. She was the organised one, the incredibly smart and diligent one. As it was, there was so much shit to untangle and deal with – including our ongoing presence at the flat. Both Usmaa and Ayesha were amazing at navigating it all – Ayesha especially. She went into Terminator mode and made a lot of really stressful and difficult decisions. I helped out and did what I could to help, but they were the real stars.

To be honest, it broke my heart. My beautiful mum becoming a widow at such a young age; my incredible sisters having to take on such a burden with precious little time to mourn; my smiley happy-go-lucky little brother losing the most important male role model in his life; and cruellest of all, sweet little Saadia, our dad's favourite who would now be without her paternal rock for her most formative years. That's what made me cry when I was alone. That's what made me bawl quietly into my pillow. I wasn't being a martyr – of course I felt sorry for myself

– but their loss is what really hurt me inside. I promised myself that I would always be there for them and do everything in my power to help them in any situation they needed me. I'd take away from their problems, instead of adding to them with my own. I'd never fall out with any of them, Inshallah, and always be their friend. I wasn't exactly the type to ever really wear my heart on my sleeve or be very open with my emotions, but I'd work hard to change that and always tell them and show them how much I cared. They could never be in any doubt that I loved them dearly and that they would *always* have someone to turn to in me. I could never in a million years replace our dad, but I could be to them what I wish I could have been to my dad – and what I wish my dad could have been to me.

Life has a funny way of staying the same for what seems like forever and then changing completely in the blink of an eye. It can happen in good ways and bad. The past and the present become so foreign to each other that they feel like different worlds. You lose people you couldn't imagine living without and find others who make the time before them seem meaningless. But there are always constants. For me, those are my faith, my family, and as sad as it seems, football. These are things you hold on to for dear life because they keep you centred and sane. In the immediate aftermath of my dad dying, I cared more about football, not less. I needed my favourite waste of time more than ever. The old, clichéd line about football being 'the most important of the unimportant things' is only a cliché because it's so true.

So I could really have done without Arsenal winning the double that season and United finishing pot-less. Lost my dad and lost the league. Thanks a bunch, Arsène. We'd been top since October and looked like we were cruising but we collapsed slowly, *achingly*, and Arsenal took full advantage. Everyone was raving about Arsène Wenger's new-fangled methods and how he was revolutionising English football for the better: mad stuff like not having a pint before kick-off. There was even talk of a new era. I wasn't sure about that. We'd played some belting football that season, but crucial injuries at the very worst times had done for us. We would still be there or thereabouts, I was sure. And even if we weren't, I could hardly complain. I'd grown up as a United fan during the most successful period in the club's history. At an age when football meant the most to me, we were pretty damn good. I could live with that. And so what if we'd replaced the greatest living human being that is Eric Cantona with Teddy Sheringham from Spurs; so what if we'd actually agreed a fee for the legitimately world-class Patrick Kluivert and ended up with Dwight fucking Yorke from Aston fucking Villa. There was always hope. There was always next season. Inshallah.

ACKNOWLEDGEMENTS

To be perfectly honest, I had so little belief in myself that I could actually finish this book that I hardly told anyone. So I'll largely stick to family, which is fitting really, seeing as this book is mostly about them.

Thank you so much to my mum Tahira; my sisters Ayesha, Usmaa and Saadia; my brother Shafiuddean; my nieces Maryam, Sara and Sophia; my nephews Abdulhameed, Ali, Saleem, Zain and Eesa; my brothers-in-law Zaiem, Nasherwan and Dawud; and my sister-in-law Shaheen.

To those of you in this book, thank you for being so patient when I pestered you for various details about our shared past (I'm sure I've misremembered so many things but I appreciate your efforts). Also, thank you for being so generous in allowing me to share them in this book. Your love and support means the world to me. Especially you, mum.

For those of you not in this book, tough! You arrived too late to be part of this particular story. But thank you, nonetheless. For so long, there were only seven of us alone. And then when dad died, only six. But seeing our family grow over the years has made me happy beyond words.

Finally, thank you to everyone at HarperNorth – but especially Jonathan de Peyer. I would not have written this book if it wasn't for you. You convinced me I had a story worth telling and the ability to tell it. You were very patient in encouraging me to do it in the first place, in spite of my self-doubts, and you were even more patient when I missed deadline after deadline. Fergie himself would be proud of how much extra time I wangled out of you.

Harper
North

BOOK CREDITS

HarperNorth would like to thank the following staff
and contributors for their involvement in making
this book a reality:

Laura Amos
Hannah Avery
Fionnuala Barrett
Luke Bird
Samuel Birkett
Claire Boal
Caroline Bovey
Ciara Briggs
Katie Buckley
Sarah Burke
Alan Cracknell
Jonathan de Peyer
Anna Derkacz
Tom Dunstan
Kate Elton
Simon Gerratt
Monica Green
Natassa Hadjinicolaou
Graham Holmes

Ben Hurd
Megan Jones
Jean-Marie Kelly
Taslima Khatun
Steve Leard
Ben McConnell
Alice Murphy-Pyle
Adam Murray
Genevieve Pegg
Agnes Rigou
James Ryan
Florence Shepherd
Zoe Shine
Emma Sullivan
Katrina Troy
Daisy Watt
Kelly Webster
Tom Whiting

For more unmissable reads,
sign up to the HarperNorth newsletter at
www.harpernorth.co.uk

or find us on Twitter at
@HarperNorthUK

**Harper
North**